DATE DUE

cast			
GAYLORD 234		PRINTED IN U.S.A.	

R
301.2   The illustrated encyclopedia of mankind.
I   London, England, Cavendish, 1974-
                    v. ill. col. maps photos.

v.20
c.1

          1. Ethnology-Dictionaries 2. Man-
Dictionaries

THE
ILLUSTRATED ENCYCLOPEDIA OF
MANKIND

Volume 20

Editor-in-chief
Richard Carlisle
Foreword: Professor C. von Fürer-Haimendorf
(formerly Dean of the School of Oriental and African Studies, London)

New edition edited and compiled by
Yvonne Deutch B.A. University of Exeter
M.A. University of Kansas, Lawrence, Kansas.

Consultant anthropologist: Michael Sallnow, London School of Economics
Preface: Professor Robert Canfield, University of Washington, St. Louis, Missouri.

MARSHALL CAVENDISH : NEW YORK, LONDON, TORONTO

Editorial Staff

EXECUTIVE EDITOR
Richard Carlisle

CONSULTANT ANTHROPOLOGIST
Andrew Barring

SENIOR EDITORS
Charles Fowkes
John Gaisford
Richard Widdows

ASSISTANT EDITORS
Christian Bailey
Thomas Browne
Mary Bryce
Donald Clarke
Francesca George
Stella Henvey
Maureen Lockhart
Hugh Peyman
Corine Plough
Oliver Robb
Noami Rowe
Robin Scagell
Jean Wetherburn

ART EDITORS
Sheila Buchanan
Steve Leaning
Gwyn Lewis
Barry Moscrop
Susan Williams
Jane Willis

DESIGNERS
Gillian Barlow
Angela Dunn

PICTURE EDITORS
Karin Magid
Kay McQueen

PICTURE RESEARCHERS
Antonia Gaunt
Jude Harris
Vanessa Thorpe

Revision Staff

CONSULTANT EDITOR
Michael Sallnow,
London School of Economics
EXECUTIVE EDITOR
Yvonne Deutch
DEPUTY EDITOR
Mary Lambert
EDITORIAL ADVISOR
Paul G. Davis
CONTRIBUTING EDITORS
Jeremy Coote, Wolfson College, Oxford
Jeanne de St Ouen, Sandy Carr
ART EDITOR
Pedro Pra Lopez
COVER DESIGN
Trevor Vertigan
PRODUCTION EXECUTIVE
Robert Paulley
PRODUCTION STAFF
Dennis Hovell, Steve Roberts

The publishers would particularly like to thank the
following contributors for their advice and guidance.

James Wilson (author of *Candian Indians,* Minority Rights Group)
Kenneth Duncan (Director of Oxfam for Latin America)
Dr. Steven Hugh-Jones (Kings College, Cambridge)
Dr. Peter Rivière (Institute of Social Anthropology, Oxford University)
Dr. André Singer (Disappearing World, Granada Television)
John Massey Stewart
Dr. Caroline Humphrey (Scott Polar Research Institute, Cambridge)
Professor C. von Fürer-Haimendorf (formerly Dean of the School
of Oriental and African Studies, University of London)
The late Professor Mervyn Jaspan (University of Hull)
Dr. C. R. Hallpike
Dr. David MacKnight (London School of Economics)
Dr. Jean La Fontaine (London School of Economics)
Dr. Phil Burnham (University College, London)

The Publishers wish to thank The Population Reference Bureau Inc. for
permission to reprint population data in Vol. 21 of the encyclopedia.

Reference Edition Published 1984
© Marshall Cavendish Limited
MCMLXXIV, MCMLXXV, MCMLXXVIII, MCMLXXXIV
Printed and bound in Italy
Published by Marshall Cavendish Corporation,
147 West Merrick Road,
Freeport,
Long Island,
N.Y. 11520

Distributed in India by Standard Literature

Library of Congress Cataloging in Publication Data

Main entry under title:

The Illustrated encyclopedia of mankind.

    Bibliography: p
    Includes index
    1. Ethnology – Dictionaries 2. Man – Dictionaries.
I   Marshall Cavendish Corporation.
GN307.144 1984   306′.03′21   84-7780
ISBN 0 86307-231-3 (Set)

ISBN 0 86307 251 8 (Vol 20)

Contents

Art and Society

The investigation of the relationship between art and society is worthwhile for two reasons. The first is that art and society are interdependent: without some kind of social organization, art would not exist. The second is that art colours our judgement of a given society even more than we ourselves realize. Our view of the ancient Greeks has been in large part created by Greek sculptures and vase-paintings; similarly, our view of early 18th century France owes much to the shimmering visions painted by Watteau. Our desire to know more about a particular society often seems to come, at least initially, from the wish to know and

The cave paintings of Lascaux are about 30,000 years old. They depict mainly hunting scenes and were probably designed to bring luck to the hunter and placate the spirit of his prey.

understand more about the works of art it has given us.

It used to be thought that the impulse to make art sprang in the first place from superfluity—that society thus consumed its own extra resources. In fact, all societies seem to have made art of some kind, however deprived or miserable their circumstances. The desire to create in this way is to be ranked with the basic necessities, like the need for nourishment and shelter.

It is easier to see the ways in which art functions in a society if we look at cultures remote from ourselves. The magnificent drawings of animals that decorate the caves used by Paleolithic peoples, for example, are probably connected with ritual magic, and this magic is in turn connected with the search for food. By making a drawing of a deer, the artist takes possession of its spirit, and very often he shows it already wounded by

spears and arrows to make certain that these will find their mark in the hunt.

Through art we trace the preoccupations of the society which produced it. We note how often artistic representations are used, not merely as a means of emphasizing what seems most important, but as a substitute for something lacking in reality. In ancient Egyptian frescoes and reliefs, for example, we very commonly encounter two different kinds of scene. We see the king vanquishing his enemies —often he is shown towering above them, enormously larger than they are. And elsewhere we find touching representations of daily life—of hunts, banquets and agricultural occupations.

The purpose of the scenes which show the king triumphant is at least threefold: they are commemorative, and serve as a memorial to a victory; they are propagandist, and make the king's subjects aware of his might; and they are pro-

(Above) The Egyptians painted their tombs with scenes of earthly pleasures which they hoped to resume in the afterlife. In this painting of about 1400BC ladies offer each other lotus blossoms.

(Below) The Parthenon Frieze showed horsemen riding in the Pan-Athenaic procession in ancient Athens. By this means both art and religion focussed citizens' loyalty on the city-state.

(Below) The Greeks and Romans adopted many Egyptian beliefs, while the Egyptians adopted the invaders' ideas of portraiture to preserve the image of their dead, as in this mummy-portrait of 140AD.

(Above right) Magnificent works of art were created during the 'Dark Ages'. This buckle was found in the Sutton Hoo burial ship, which was equipped for the afterlife of a 7th century Anglo-Saxon king.

(Right) Indian miniature painting reached its peak between the 16th and 19th centuries. Subjects chosen reflected the sumptuous life of the few, like this prince who strolls with his favourite in a garden.

phylactic, and serve to ward off defeat upon some future occasion. The scenes of daily life, on the other hand, appear in connection with the cult of the dead. They are meant to ensure that the pleasures of this life will be continued in the next, that the status of the dead man will be preserved, and that he will find himself surrounded by everything he has been accustomed to enjoy.

The pattern of particular societies in the ancient world emerges vividly from the works of art they have left us. The long processions of guards and tribute-bearers carved in relief at Persepolis speak of the despotism of the Great King of Persia, and of the power exercised by one man. On the other hand, the frieze from the Parthenon in Athens, though it too shows a procession, is about something altogether different. It shows the whole city moving towards the gods, and in particular towards the goddess who personifies the *polis*, or city-state. The community makes homage to itself.

One of the more important functions of art, however, is to take the human being beyond anything he knows in objective reality. The work of art serves as the mediator between man and his gods. We see this clearly in Christian art; and we see, too, how the artist responds to the religious climate of feeling, as well as to the dogma he seeks to express. Among the most powerful religious images ever produced are Byzantine representations of Christ, such as the one in the dome of the church of Daphni in Greece. The ruler of the world blesses but also seems to threaten his worshippers, as he looks down at them from on high. Quite different are the graceful statues of the Virgin produced in France and Germany during the late Middle Ages. These speak of a more intimate and comforting faith, an easier transition from the worshipper to the worshipped.

But the Christian artist does far more than provide the images which serve as a focus for devotion. He renders the stories of the Old and the New Testament, and the legends of the saints, inside the church itself—this was of great importance where the congregation was illiterate. Outstanding examples are the stained glass windows in Canterbury Cathedral, some of which tell the story of the martyred St Thomas à-Becket; and the cycle of frescoes in Assisi, by Giotto and his assistants, which illustrate scenes from the life of St Francis. The painted and sculptured decoration of medieval churches does more than illustrate sacred texts: it suggests the existence of a moral order.

Christianity is not alone among the world's religions in employing art to mediate and to teach. Buddhist and Hindu temples are at least as elaborate from this point of view as the cathedrals of Europe. What perhaps tends to mark Christian art off from that produced by other faiths is the part played by style.

It is typical of religious art to follow a fixed and traditional scheme. The artist finds merit in repeating what is prescribed; the image draws its effectiveness from close adherence to a traditional pattern. The Russian icon-painters worked in this way for many centuries. But even during the Middle Ages, and certainly afterwards, Christian painters and sculptors engaged in a dialogue with their subject-matter which left them free

The Wilton Diptych shows King Richard II of England being presented to the Virgin Mary by his patron saints. In the Late Middle Ages the wealth and power of such royal connoisseurs gave them greater individual importance. It also allowed them to use art to claim religious support for political dominance.

to change and vary traditional formulations. This leads us to consider the style of a work of art—not merely what it seems to say, but the manner in which it says it.

We can understand the importance of this question by looking at a specific work. The Christ of the Isenheim Altarpiece, by Grunewald, is just one of thousands of late medieval representations of the Crucifixion. Yet it is the only one which strikes this particular note of horror and pathos. The laceration of the body and the writhing limbs convey a quite special emotion, and the style of the work is only partly explained when we learn that the picture was painted for a hospital chapel: that the sick were brought into its presence in the hope that the violence of the image would either drive out the disease or purge their souls so that they could accept their own approaching end. We note this, but at the

Cooper-Bridgeman/National Gallery

enable him to commission so exquisite a work of art.

Once this stage had been reached, it was possible to dispense with the religious element. In the Arnolfini Wedding, by the same artist, the search for status is unabashed. The prosperous young Italian merchant and his wife who appear in the picture want to show us not only who they were but how they lived, what clothes they wore, what possessions surrounded them.

It is sometimes assumed that realism of this type is the true aim of the artist—that works of art which are not realistic in some sense fall short of the artist's intention. This belief was held much more widely during the 19th century, before many Europeans had been exposed to cultures which lay outside their own tradition. The realistic impulse is, however, a strangely spasmodic phenomenon, often connected with the desire to make convincing portraits: we find this among the Hellenistic Greeks and the Romans, in the ancestor portraits of the Chinese and Japanese, in a group of heads from Ife in West Africa, and in much post-Renaissance European art.

Absence of realism can spring from a number of causes. The first is that our eyes and minds are not adjusted to the system of artistic conventions employed in the particular work. There is every reason to suppose, for example, that the visual 'code' which appears in ancient Egyptian paintings and reliefs seemed acceptably realistic to the original audience. Secondly, and far more important, the various departures from realism can be connected with their social purpose.

Good examples of this are the expressive distortions and transformations which we find in African masks or in Aztec sculptures. Though the departures from the norm are not in our eyes so violent, there are also significant departures from realism in European works such as the Marie de Medicis cycle by Rubens and the frescoes by G. B. Tiepolo at Wurzburg. The series of paintings by Rubens are a simpler case than the comparable cycle by Tiepolo. Rubens uses allegory to glorify his patron, who appears surrounded by various mythological figures and transported into situations for which no parallel can be found in ordinary life. What we find in these works is the status game being played full out. Everything we see conspires to impress us with the virtue and the power of the royal personage.

Tiepolo, too, makes use of allegory, but adds an element of illusion—that is, he tricks the eye into seeing things which the brain knows cannot exist. The dream world into which he transports the spectator is not realistic in the manner of a work by Van Eyck. The 'beyond' into which he lures us is not the mirror of the

same time recognize that the artist has found room to make a purely personal statement about his own relationship to the godhead.

In the secular sphere, one of the most important functions of art has been to mark the degrees of social relationships and to emphasize differences in status. This secular task can quite easily be intermingled with a religious purpose. We find it happening in the European Middle Ages, when religion penetrated every aspect of everyday life. The Wilton Diptych, now in the National Gallery in London, is a portable altarpiece which shows King Richard II of England being presented to the Virgin by his patron

saints. Here everything suggests an identification between royalty and religion —the king is exalted into the sacred sphere, and the implication is that the royal personage thus presented to us is in many important respects different from the ordinary mortals over whom he rules.

An interesting contrast in a similar composition is the Madonna of Chancellor Rollin, by Jan Van Eyck. Here the mechanism is quite different: it is the Virgin who descends into the secular sphere, to confront the kneeling donor. The aim here is not to impress us with a difference in nature between Chancellor Rollin and ourselves, but with a difference in wealth and power—the things which

life we know, but something more dynamic and irrational. Beneath its irrationality, however, there still lies the steady purpose of raising the prestige of the patron.

We must not assume that all art which interests itself in status is extrovert in the manner of the two examples described. Art is often used not so much as a means of impressing the spectator with the power or wealth of the patron as for drawing a distinction between groups, for distinguishing the 'insiders' from those who are excluded. One of the most interesting phenomena in European art, for instance, is the recurrence of a 'court style' at various times and in various places, which can sometimes take deceptive forms.

Today we delight in the scenes of peasant life painted by the Limbourg brothers for their patron Jean, Duke of Berri. They seem to give us a complete panorama of rural occupations in the early 15th century. What is not always realized is that these scenes were painted on the assumption that they would seem almost as remote and exotic to the original patron as they do to us. The same is true of the peasant scenes of Pieter Breughel the Elder. His patrons were men from the highest level of society, who found reassurance in what was so far from their own way of life.

The court style later became more complex. The artists of the school of Fontainebleau, who worked for Francis I of France and his successors, came from all over Europe and owed loyalty only to the court and its tastes. Their work is intricate and full of riddles and hidden images; if the spectator did not know the secrets, he remained on the outside. Still later, at the beginning of the 18th century, Antoine Watteau invented a fantasy of escape: the *fête galante*, which showed elegant people amusing themselves in idealized situations, highly refined and with a subtle nostalgia. The spectator was offered a refuge from the harsh realities of the everyday world, the implication being that he was too delicate a spirit to

(Above) The 11th century mosaic of Christ Pantocrator in the monastery dome at Daphni, near Athens, impressed the worshipper with the Byzantine concept of a God who is to be feared as well as loved.

(Left) In the Middle Ages the vast majority of people could not read, and Christian artists used their skills to bring Bible stories alive. This 12th-century stained glass is from Canterbury Cathedral.

(Left) Realism in art has appeared in many different periods and places, and for varied reasons. This beautiful bronze head was made at Ife, in what is now Nigeria, perhaps in the 13th century.

(Right) The rich and powerful merchant patrons of 15th century Flanders demanded an art which reflected their success in this world. In this portrait of Arnolfini and his wife, the couple are surrounded by symbols of prosperity, fertility and a happy marriage. The artist, Jan van Eyck, appears in the mirror on the back wall.

C. M. Dixon

Michael Holford

Werner Foreman Archive/British Museum

survive without the solace offered by the artist.

The notion of art as a refuge is widespread; a parallel to some of Watteau's paintings is offered by scenes depicted in Indian miniatures of the 17th, 18th and early 19th century. The patrons here were the Moghul rulers and the lesser Rajahs who imitated them, and the subjects are often idyllic scenes of girls dallying in gardens or sporting with their lovers.

Similar attitudes are expressed in Chinese and Japanese art, but in a somewhat different way. In Japan the cult of the tea-ceremony taught the rich and powerful to appreciate the beauty of humble objects, and particularly that of the rough earthenware tea-bowls which were passed from hand to hand. The implications of the tea-ceremony were religious—it had, and has, a close connection with Zen Buddhism. But one can also see in it a subtle exclusivity and assertion of social power: the person who can afford any luxury is the very one who can afford to express admiration for that which is humble and simple.

In China, from the Sung Dynasty onwards, the appreciation of art and the right to make it became the preserve of the scholar-intellectuals who governed the Chinese empire. Chinese painting is closely linked to the Chinese method of writing, which used a brush instead of a

In the 17th century the idea of the Divine Right of Kings was often questioned. Monarchs used art for propaganda, as in Ruben's painting of the Coronation of Marie de Medici, the wife of Henry IV of France.

pen. Anyone who could write Chinese characters elegantly was already equipped to be a painter, and as a result it was the non-professional painter whose work was the most respected, and a capacity to make art became one of the distinguishing marks of the ruling group.

The paintings themselves expressed a carefully cultivated refinement of sensibility—panoramic landscapes in which there meditated the tiny figure of a sage, or flowers and stems of bamboo. The very format spoke of the desire for exclusivity. Painted on scrolls, the works were kept rolled up, and were brought out to be enjoyed in the company of a few congenial friends.

In China and also in Japan, the business of collecting art soon became important. To own, and therefore control, the work of the artist became crucial in the search for status; and to this was added an elaborate cult of the connoisseur.

We meet a similar phenomenon in the West; and we also meet it among primitive peoples in a different but recognizable form. Perhaps the earliest reason for wishing to own objects which were of no practical use—which could not be eaten, worn, or used as tools—sprang from the conviction that there were some things which, though apparently useless, gave power or comfort to the possessor.

Works of art have often been desired for their intrinsic value as well as for their aesthetic merit. We must, however, realise that the very notion of 'intrinsic value' is itself based on a convention— the near-universal agreement, for example, that gold is a valuable substance. Another reason for wishing to possess a work of art is that it serves as a

specimen of demonstration of the artist's skill. Patrons or collectors look for what is most skilfully made. They have a competitive desire to demonstrate their own acumen, and to possess and command: the skill they purchase becomes, as it were, their own.

When we look at the impulse to collect, we see that one of the outstanding functions of art has always been to 'enlarge' to create a sense of significance for us and our surroundings. There is obviously, a great difference in the way this is achieved in different cultures. The art of ancient civilizations, and that produced in primitive cultures, tends to remain relatively fixed. Its part in religious or secular rituals is easy to define, and so is the position of the artist in relation to his subject. In primitive societies we may notice a stylistic progression, a gradual alteration of forms, but these changes are so slow as to imply a kind of timelessness.

The art of the West is quite different in this respect, and this applies especially to post-Renaissance art. The thing which seems to divide Western society most sharply from others is the great emphasis which the West places upon individuality, and the perpetual awareness of a conflict between the individual and the collective mass. It often seems as if the visual arts supply one of the most important arenas in which this conflict is acted out. In any case, it is certain that the art produced by our own culture has long been involved with the consciousness of self. This has often led critics to feel that Western art cannot be interpreted in a sociological sense at all. A later examination of Western art questions this assumption. □

Early European Art

Scala

The art produced in Europe from the fall of the Roman Empire until the dawn of the Renaissance is sometimes spoken of as if it formed a unity. In fact, while its geographical homogeneity is often impressive, the art of this period is extremely varied, and the variations we see in it accurately reflect successive stages of social development.

The first phase is that of the so-called Dark Ages. In the West, though not in the East, Graeco-Roman civilization was overwhelmed by successive waves of barbarian migration. What the barbarians brought with them was old-fashioned in comparison to what they found—it resembled the work produced by the tribes whom the Romans had conquered in Gaul and elsewhere. It was an art of warrior nomads, and its typical products were finely decorated arms, and small articles of personal adornment for both men and women, such as belt buckles and brooches. The decoration itself consisted of intricate abstract patterns—a negation of everything that classical art, with its concentration on the

This mosaic at Ravenna, showing the Court of Justinian, is an example of early Christian Byzantine art. In ceremonial, organization and art, Court and Church imitated each other.

human figure, had stood for.

At the same time the classical ideal found itself being attacked from another direction. The rise of Christianity also tended to devalue traditional artistic ideals. Christianity stood for the spirit rather than the flesh; and certainly in the days when it was still officially persecuted, it was anti-luxurious.

When the Emperor Constantine at last bestowed imperial patronage upon the Christians, this naturally began to change, and the Empire of the East, with its capital at the new metropolis of Constantinople, was soon to evolve an art which mirrored the political and religious realities of the Byzantine state. The Emperor was God's representative on earth, and church and court ceremonials became to some extent interchangeable.

Byzantine art aimed to reproduce the spiritual reality, rather than what the eyes perceived, and this is the reason for some of its characteristic formal devices. One of the most notable of these is the so-called 'reverse perspective', by which the important figures in a composition are always represented as being larger than the others, whether or not they are farther away.

In the West, barbarian conquest was followed by economic breakdown, and a new pattern of life emerged. Trade stagnated, and life was increasingly lived on large, self-sufficient country estates and not in cities. Much reduced in importance, the towns survived for the most part as the seats of bishoprics. The new Empire established by Charlemagne, in the late 8th and early 9th century, was very different from the Roman Empire it had replaced. Yet it had a real nostalgia for this predecessor, and it is in Carolingian times that we meet the first of the 'classical revivals' which have marked the history of European art.

The re-affirmation of classical values

Michael Holford/British Museum

Michael Holford/Prado

(Above left) This fibula from Sutton Hoo was used to pin the clothing of an Anglo-Saxon chief. The use of gold and the elaborate strapwork ornamentation are typical of Northern European art in the 'Dark Ages'.

(Left) The mysticism of Medieval Christianity is reflected in this painting of Paradise, a panel from The Garden of Earthly Delights, by Bosch. But the personal attitude of the artist is unmistakable.

served only to mark the distance which the Carolingians had travelled from the Romans. Despite a renewed interest in the human figure, this was not a monumental art. Its characteristic products were carved ivories and book-illumination, and these have the delicate refinement characteristic of court taste in all cultures. Though most of the objects which have survived were designed for ecclesiastical use, there is no element of the popular about them. They were clearly designed for the pleasure of a tiny élite.

The next phase in the development of European art was the Romanesque. The court was no longer the only cultural and intellectual centre, and the initiative shifted to the monasteries. One reason for this was their increasing wealth; an even stronger one was the greater continuity of monastic life, as opposed to the perpetual changes of fortune which affected laymen. In the monasteries, the aristocratic prejudice against manual

labour was overcome, as the rule under which the monks lived prescribed that they should undertake physical as well as intellectual occupations. The visual arts ceased to be entirely the business of the low-born artisan, and the regular pattern of monastic existence led to the establishment of properly organized workshops.

The transition from Romanesque to early Gothic is the story of increasing intellectual as well as practical organization. In some respects the great churches built in the !1th century seem at odds with the carvings that adorn them. Where the buildings are severe and apparently regular in their proportions, the carvings show us a phantasmagoric world of monsters and demons; and even the representation of the human figure is sometimes marked by what now seems a frantic expressionism. In fact, these two tendencies are more easily reconciled than looks likely at first. Romanesque buildings, though regular, are not unified; they are collections of parts. The sculptures, too, reflect the same lack of overall intellectual discipline. The medieval mind is not yet sure of the boundaries that govern its world.

These boundaries were eventually supplied by the growth of medieval scholasticism, and the birth of Gothic represents the increasing control achieved by medieval theologians. It was natural that the achievements of this third phase, as we find it represented in buildings such as Chartres Cathedral and Saint-Denis, should be concerned above all with the achievement of unity.

We next meet a style in which the unity sought for is abstract, and where its effect is purely aesthetic. This is the developed Gothic of elaborate pattern. As if to stress the way in which art was falling out of step with social needs, we also find a counter-current which moved in a very different direction. At Rheims Cathedral, some of the statues show a classicizing tendency, which is echoed only a little later by the frescoes painted by Giotto for the Arena Chapel in Padua.

In Germany, there is an even more unexpected development, typified by the mid-13th century statues of founders or 'watchers' in the west choir of Naumburg Cathedral. The realism of these figures— aggressive but not grotesque—is something entirely new in Gothic art. In the 13th and 14th century the visual arts suddenly make us aware of a new complexity in European society.

But society itself was not yet ready to acknowledge the changes which were taking place. What we most naturally associate with this phase of medieval civilization is not the isolated achievement of the sculptors at Rheims and Naumburg, but the International Gothic style, which was by its very nature incapable of such intensity. The purpose of the International Gothic seems to be to defend the spectator from dangerous emotions, to wrap him in a pleasant dream world where everything will forever be the same.

At the culmination of the style, around the year 1400, the International Gothic had spread to every country in Europe, and we recognize in it the strenuous efforts of the old aristocratic society to maintain itself, and its conventions and values, in the face of a social upheaval from below. In the place of an almost static society, with a sluggish economic life, we now find a dynamic social organism where trade has given birth to densely populated urban communities, especially in the Low Countries and in Northern Italy.

In Italy, medieval ideals had already for some time been challenged by those of the intellectual revolution we now call the Renaissance. In Flanders a powerful merchant class had replaced the Medieval

Scala

(*Above*) *Four centuries after the collapse of Rome, Charlemagne revived the idea of empire in Europe. His tomb is an example of an art which imitated the classical for functional as well as aesthetic reasons, but was used to decorate more intimate objects.*

(*Right*) *The legend of St George and the Dragon was a common subject of late mediaeval paintings, because it provided a ready symbol for the ideas of courtly love.*

The work of this period represents perhaps the most impressive achievement of the medieval artist. A complete world view had evolved, and we find it symbolized by the way every part of a given artistic enterprise is made to relate to all the other parts. The famous statues which adorn the west portals of Chartres, for example, are like columns in more than one sense—we are made to feel that the architectural figure has quite spontaneously taken on human form.

The Gothic art of this phase represents a kind of equilibrium within society itself. The whole social mass is animated by the same faith, and all its members direct their efforts towards the same ends. Soon, however, the balance began to shift again, and the direction in which it moved was towards increasing secularization. The spiritual unity of the early Gothic could not be maintained at the same level, and the artist gradually became obsessed with his own virtuosity.

Michael Holford/Victoria & Albert Museum

aristocracy as patrons, and the art which they commissioned was startlingly different from anything that had preceded it. It was intensely realistic, and the artists' aim was to translate everything into strictly contemporary terms.

When Dirc Bouts was commissioned to produce a painting of the Last Supper, he showed the meal taking place in a setting which would have been recognizable immediately to any member of his audience. The picture is a wonderfully detailed document which tells us everything we might wish to know about the interior decoration and furnishing of the time. The aim was to make the truths of the Christian religion tangible and accessible in a way that they had never been before. At the same time the picture becomes a tragic mirror in which a world is preserved for eternity.

The prosaic quality of a painting such as this contrasts curiously with the extreme mystical emotion of other works of the same period. The illuminations in the *Heures de Rohan*, for example, seem to belong to a universe totally alien to that which produced the picture by Bouts, though they date from only 30 years or so earlier. The famous Avignon *Pieta* in the Louvre is probably almost exactly

contemporary with the *Last Supper*. Here, too, we are conscious of a huge gulf of style, yet the intentions of these different artists are not so far apart: they all aim to make religion speak in a direct and personal way.

The chief impression we receive from the closing phase of medieval art is one of violent psychological strain, of a society painfully at odds with itself. The mysticism of the time was a direct reaction to the situation in which men found themselves. The old assumptions about the world, built up over the cen-

(Left) The statues of the Saints at Chartres Cathedral are part of the architectural structure. The best Gothic art was an integral part of the whole composition.

(Right) Book illumination remained an important art form even after the invention of printing. It received a great impetus during the 'Dark Ages', when the copying of books by hand was raised to a fine art in the monasteries. This late example, c1418 AD, is from the Rohan Book of Hours, and depicts a dying man commending his soul to God.

turies from Charlemagne onwards, were beginning to dissolve. In the work of a artist from the very end of the medieval tradition—Hieronimus Bosch—we find a world as grotesque as that sometimes shown to us in Romanesque carving. Yet the disturbing thing about Bosch's *Earthly Paradise* is less the grotesquerie of various images than the sense of a secret organization uniting them, whose pattern we cannot quite grasp.

In Bosch we feel the growth of a special sense of individuality, unconnected with any philosophical system, though these would soon grow up to account for it. The medieval artist, despite the changes of stylistic orientation, remains less an artist in our contemporary sense than a craftsman who performs a set task. The aim he sets himself to fulfil is clearly understood from the beginning, and very often artists received absolutely specific instructions from those who employed them. While it is not true to say that medieval artists were content to be anonymous (many of them signed their work), they were satisfied with the fame that comes from a job well done. But by the end of the period, the artist begins to claim the right to speak as himself and for himself. ☐

Bulloz

Snark/Bibliothèque Nationale

Later European Art

Sociologists and art historians often protest at the use of the Renaissance as a dividing line. They argue that the gulf between the early and the late Middle Ages was probably more profound than that which exists between the late Middle Ages and what followed them. Yet the old division has a certain validity. In particular, it draws our attention to certain aspects of European art which make it very different from the art produced by other cultures.

The most conspicuous of these differences is the European attitude towards human individuality, that emphasis which we place upon the qualities and attributes which isolate the individual from the social mass. This is not to say that other cultures show no perception of the different traits which go to make up a recognizable personality. Portraiture has a long and honourable history; we find naturalistic portraits among the ancient Egyptians, in Africa and among the Chinese and Japanese.

The Western tradition of portraiture, however, stems from Graeco-Roman civilization, and in particular from the Hellenistic age. From this it runs, almost unbroken, through the Dark Ages and through the centuries of medieval art. The likenesses of the medieval French and English kings are, for example, preserved in a long sequence of tomb effigies.

By the first half of the 15th century portraits of unrivalled vividness were being produced by professional artists almost as a matter of course. The most significant development, however, was the rise of the self-portrait, for there is an important difference between commissioning a likeness and making one's own likeness oneself. The person who commissions a portrait may only be asserting a sense of their own importance; the artist painting a self-portrait is inevitably engaged in an act of self-examination which stretches beyond the mere details of appearance. Dürer's self-portraits, for example, are not only typical products of the Renaissance, but signify the new role which was now to be claimed by the European artist.

From the self-portrait it was a short step to as revolutionary new attitude. The work of art began to be thought of as the mirror of the artist's individuality, what-

In the various unfinished pieces by Michelangelo, such as this Pieta, the human form seems to emerge from the stone as though it were waiting there to be uncovered.

Photoresources

ever its ostensible subject-matter. While it took some time for this to become the primary consideration in the spectator's reaction to the work of art, it was certainly present from the Renaissance onwards. As a result the artist came to occupy a social position at once more mobile and more ambiguous than that accorded to him in most cultures.

The social mobility of artists had

existed even in the hierarchical society of the Middle Ages. When John II, King of France, was taken prisoner at the battle of Crecy, his favourite painter, Girart d'Orleans, followed him into captivity in England. Household accounts make it clear that Girart was valued as a companion, as well as for his professional skills. On the whole, however, medieval artists were bound by the guild system which governed the lives of all artisans.

There is a tremendous contrast between the situation of even a Girart d'Orleans and that which contemporaries accorded to Michelangelo. Girart was a king's favourite, and Michelangelo the familiar

lizations. Though the artist to some extent continues to serve recognized social ends—as a teacher, illustrator of status and of social boundaries, and so forth—he also performs a series of quite different tasks, whose social relevance is less immediately recognizable.

The artist becomes, for example, the recognized critic, almost the enemy, of society, the one who constantly reminds others that the individual has value apart from the mass. Paradoxically, artists sometimes need to form a kind of 'anti-society' of their own, in order to do this. A subject which is still inadequately explored is the way in which the medieval guild system was gradually transformed into what we should now call Bohemia.

As any reader of Francois Villon's poems will know, the social world of the Middle Ages was not without Bohemian elements of its own—a class of outcasts and outlaws who banded together in order to resist authority. But the Bohemian world only seems to take on coherent and recognizable form with the

(Left) **One of Rembrandt's later self-portraits records the face of an artist whose popularity had deserted him, although he was still highly regarded as a craftsman. Self-knowledge had come with old age but also disillusionment.**

(Below) **David's Oath of the Horatii was painted in 1784–85, and established the artist's reputation. It was intended not for the aristocracy but for the educated middle class, which understood the classical allusion as a call-to-arms in pre-revolutionary France.**

Louvre/Michael Holford

companion of popes, but there all resemblance ceases. As the lives written by Vasari and Condivi make plain, Michelangelo was thought of as a wholly exceptional being, exempt from all rules, able to pit his own genius against the worldly power and financial resources of those who paid him to work for them. Indeed, these 16th century accounts of the greatest of contemporary artists give us a good picture of the emergence of the idea of 'genius' in the abstract.

Certain artists were now regarded as exemplary, because they gave the rest of humanity a new and larger idea of the powers inherent in one person. The work of art, instead of being simply the result and justification of the process of making it, became also the outward symbol, the inadequate embodiment, of the magic the genius held within himself.

By the 17th century, certain patterns had started to emerge in European art which are similar to those we see in the art of our own day, and different from those to be found in that of other civi-

Louvre/Michael Holford

great influx of artists from the Low Countries to Italy in the 16th and particularly the 17th century. These artists were cut off from the world in which they had been born, and did not become assimilated to the world in which they found themselves.

Instead they formed a society within a society, conspicuous for the delight which it took in flouting the rules of 'respectable' life, and equipped with its own rituals. At the same time, the economics of painting changed. Instead of working on commission, these Italo-Flemish artists usually worked for stock, and marketed what they painted through dealers. The client could accept or reject the finished product, but he exercised no direct influence over its content.

We can gauge the effects of this by looking at the careers of painters whose fierce individuality separates them even from the 'anti-society' of Bohemia, though they have some superficially Bohemian characteristics. In Italy, Salvator Rosa 'the painter of banditti' identified himself with the outlaws who swarmed around the peninsula, as well as taking them for his subject-matter. At the same time, he made himself a reputation as poet, philosopher and conversationalist. It is clear that his most important creation was not his paintings but his persona, and that this persona was a

self-conscious critique of his surroundings.

But if there is something theatrical and superficial about Rosa, which limits the value of his art, we cannot make the same comment about Rembrandt. While it is clear that consciousness of self was one of the mainsprings of Rembrandt's activity, with him we must strip the adjective 'self-conscious' of all its usually perjorative overtones.

Do we add to our knowledge of either art or society by trying to put work of this kind into a sociological context? If we look at him simply as a Dutch artist, working in a particular kind of bourgeois society, painting for a market which eventually deserted him, we achieve little of this. What is significant and moving is the sense of disharmony with his context which Rembrandt conveys to us. For example, tracing the series of self-portraits from beginning to end, we note the physical degeneration and the loss of social confidence as well as the increase in self-knowledge they convey. Our idea of 17th century Holland would be very different if the only Dutch painters we knew were the group who slavishly reflect the minutiae of the domestic interior and the tavern.

The art of the 18th century seems in many respects more conservative than that of the 17th, with less emphasis upon individualism. Fragonard was content to

Turner's Rain, Steam and Speed is an essay in light which, like the later Impressionist paintings, records a moment in a constantly changing scene.

mythologize the relationship between Louis XV and his mistress, Mme Dubarry; Stubbs was happy to portray the horses of the English gentry. What was new at this period was the growth of art theory. The *Discourses* of Sir Joshua Reynolds and the *Salons* of Diderot are landmarks in this process.

Diderot is especially important because he was a man looking at painting from the outside, not a professional artist. He applied to the visual arts the ideas and the intellectual standards of the 18th century Enlightenment. In some respects the results were not happy; art, instead of functioning naturally within a society, now had a mission imposed upon it. The artist's duty was to be a moralist.

Jacques Louis David is an especially important figure in the history of post-Renaissance art because we see in him both the opportunities and the dangers which confront the painter who deliberately commits himself to a social role. *The Oath of the Horatii*, the picture which made David's reputation, was not merely an echo of the turmoil which was beginning to shake French society, it was designed to increase that turmoil and to direct its energies.

The Death of Marat is not just a personal cry of grief; it is a revolutionary icon, designed to bring together and give form to the emotions of the mass. Yet one of the lessons of David's career is that the artist assumes the role of spokesman to the peril of his art. The cold rhetoric of the pictures which David painted to exalt the Napoleonic régime is worlds away from the humanity of Rembrandt.

The reaction against David and his school brought with it an art which committed itself to the portrayal of subjective feeling. A Romantic artist such as Delacroix will often seem to reject any duty society may lay on him, in order to pursue his own fantasies. His pleasure often lies in stressing the distance which separates him, as a creator, from the rest of his fellows.

The cross-currents within the 19th century visual arts are exceptionally complex. We find the artist, in the mid-century, with Courbet and Millet, picking up the notion of social responsibility where David had left it. With the English Pre-Raphaelites and the German Nazarenes, we find him trying to provide an escape from the horrors of the industrial milieu. We also find him, with the Impressionists, mildly flirting with science, and trying to analyze appearance in a way which is at least pseudo-scientific. None of these tendencies changes the basic line of development, which continues to put more and more emphasis on the idea of art as something gratuitous, an expression of free-will in an increasingly confined and constricting environment.

From the Romanticism of Delacroix it is really only a short distance to the so-called Modern Movement of the present century, which takes up a number of the earlier ideas about art and the artist and presents them in a new way. Part of the myth of modernism is that it is necessary for artists to go so far beyond the artistic and even the social conventions of their time that society is bound to reject them. It is only after this symbolic act of rejection that they can be accepted again, first by their peers—their fellow-artists— then, gradually, by a repentant public.

S.P.A.D.E.M. Paris 1975/Giraudon/Museum of Modern Art

Picasso's Les Demoiselles d'Avignon (1906–7) was one of the first Cubist pictures. The portrait of a group of prostitutes conveys the artist's attitude towards them, as well as attempting to analyze the shapes beneath the surface of what the eye actually sees. Cubism followed from Impressionism and was the beginning of abstract art.

The impact of a painting could be startling in ages before the mass media. By contrast, a 20th century artist such as Roy Lichtenstein has a vast range of cultural ephemera to interpret. The viewer has to decide whether or not a comic strip is to be considered as art.

Picasso's *Demoiselles d'Avignon* marks the beginning of Cubism, and is therefore one of the key monuments of modern art. At the time it was painted, its subject was ugliness. The audience was supposed to be horrified by its outright rejection of everything that was previously thought beautiful. The dialogue was soon to be continued by the Dadaists, an *avant-garde* group who proclaimed themselves as being, quite simply, 'anti-art'.

In its essentials, the debate between art and non-art has continued ever since, and the ambition of each succeeding generation of artists has been, as the Pop artist Roy Lichtenstein said in the 1960s, 'to paint a picture that nobody would hang'. The dynamic of 20th century art is based on the assumption that there is always some frontier the creator must cross, or go beyond, and that unless he does so his work is valueless. In some ways this is merely a response to the pressures of commercialism, but we are also justified in thinking of this as a crude version of that search for the transcendental which has haunted European art intermittently since the birth of Christianity. A materialist society has been forced to reformulate the 'beyond' in a way that does not violate its own materialism. But in another way we can think of it more positively, as part of the effort to extend our idea of what a person is. ☐

Tate Gallery London/Chris Barker

I PRESSED THE FIRE CONTROL...AND AHEAD OF ME ROCKETS BLAZED THROUGH THE SKY

WHAAM!

Art of the Amerindians

Despite the great diversity in the social structure of Amerindian tribes, there is an underlying unity in their art. They show a preference for surface decoration with a symbolic meaning. They tend to avoid realism in favour of pattern-making, and they exhibit a love for bright colours. Within their societies there is usually considerable respect paid to the quality of work, so the skilled artist is a person whose work is treasured.

Among Amerindians in general, body decoration is common: tattooing in a few cases, but everywhere body painting in strongly marked designs is a means of self-expression. In many tribes the individual felt himself to be under the protection of a spirit being, often of animal form. This relationship was expressed in personal painting, and in the carvings and paintings of the home and clothing. This spirit protector was called a 'totem' (a Chippewa Indian term used by anthropologists nowadays for all such symbolic concepts). The clans within a tribe had their group totems, which were often regarded as ancestors in animal form.

The purpose of artistic craftsmanship could be simply decorative; or magical, to ensure the protection of the spirit-world; or historical, to record a chieftain's achievements and tribal history. This historical function of art is confined to the more organized societies where certain families became a kind of aristocracy. In a few cases a system of written records evolved, but this was in a limited area of high civilization in Mexico and Peru.

The natives of Tierra del Fuego (among the most unsophisticated artistically), used to paint themselves with red and white, and made bark masks to impersonate their protective spirits. They did no other truly artistic work, though their tools and weapons were well made.

The Indians of the Pampas were hunters and also painted themselves. At first they wore the skins of the wild guanaco llama, but after European contacts they made great robes of horse and cow hide. These they decorated with geometric patterns in red, white and yellow. The robes were worn by all, but especially splendid ones were envied.

Similarly, far to the north the Eskimo wore fine fur clothing, made by the women from many different skins, with great decorative effect. Most of the Eskimo

carried hunting charms to bring luck. These little birds and seals carved from walrus tusks are very beautiful, but their purpose was for magic. Some of the animal ribs used for bow drills were engraved with scenes of daily life for decoration, and many wooden objects, such as the masks worn by *shamans*, were painted. Canoe paddles were sometimes decorated with pictures of happiness in the spirit world.

The Indian hunters of the Canadian forests spent most of their artistic talent in decorating clothing and painting their faces. A few made wooden figures of their protective spirits and these were sometimes accompanied by strings on which objects had been knotted as reminders of past events. Like the Eskimo and the South American hunters, they had no chiefs of importance, just sensible men who took on the leadership of the band

A Peruvian stirrup-vase, dating from early in the Christian era, depicts a man with a small pouch for coca leaves. Pottery is still one of the major art forms of the Amerindians.

Michael Holford

from time to time.

But along the forested Pacific Coast from Oregon to Alaska there lived several tribes who had no agriculture and subsisted by fishing and hunting. They lived in big wooden houses, under the rule of clan chiefs. They excelled in craftsmanship, using stone tools to cut wood, which they decorated with ceremonial carvings. These tribes were also skilled at grinding stone into shapes of pestles and mortars. Everything they made was dedicated to the totemic spirits of the tribe. The finest things were made for the chiefs, including beautiful twined blankets in patterns of white, blue and yellow.

In the winter there were dances relating stories of the totem ancestors of the clans. The actors wore painted masks, representing birds and animals as well as human beings. In modern times they carved huge totem poles because they had obtained steel tools from the Whites, but even in the old days house posts were carved and house walls painted. The purpose of this was to please the spirits and to glorify the clan and its chief. The totem poles showed which clan the members of the house belonged to and supported, and promised help to any clansman who called there.

These Indians of the Pacific Coast practised an elaborate festival called the *potlatch*, a Chinook word meaning 'give-away', at which great amounts of their art and craft production would be distributed. There were various occasions for these, but most involved validating a man's claim to certain rights: on the death of a chief, for instance, his successor would host a *potlatch*.

Some tribes had a face-saving *potlatch*, by means of which a man could redeem his dignity after something embarrasing had happened to him. A chief had to give away an amount of goods according to his rank, and the value of the goods received was determined by the social position of the recipient, who was required to give away more than he had received when it was his turn to perform a *potlatch* ceremony. There were competitive *potlatches*, in which competitors for social position vied with each other, even to the point of destroying goods.

A complex financial structure grew up to support the system, including interest-bearing loans. The *potlatch* tradition sur-

John Hemming

(*Above*) *Body painting is the only form of artistic expression used by the Xikrin Indians of Brazil—they make neither pottery nor sculpture. They begin painting their children's bodies as soon as they are born, and renew it every 10 or 12 days.*

(*Below*) *Tlinglit Indians carve a totem pole at Port Chilkoot, Alaska. Totem poles have become more elaborate since the introduction of metal tools, but houseposts have long been carved to identify the clan.*

Bartlett/Colorific!

The Indians of Central and South America were famous for their skilled work in gold. This Peruvian funerary mask, made about 1200 AD, was inlaid with emeralds and shows traces of red paint.

vived until the 1950s, and was revived in the 1970s by which time the Indians were giving goods to each other, such as motorboats and colour television sets; originally, the festivals served the economic function of distributing the tribes' goods, as well as a social function.

The eastern United States was also a region of high artistic endeavour. In the north the Iroquois made much fine work in wood and bone, but they also made patterned belts of purple and white beads from the hinge joints of a shellfish. These beaded belts were called *wampum*, and were made up into patterned bands which were reminders of events. Once a year the belts were taken out and 'read' by the Keepers of the *Wampum* who remembered the stories belonging to each belt.

Further south the tribes were carvers in wood; some particularly beautiful masks have been excavated in Florida. Along the Ohio River, at the beginning of the Christian era, Indians made great artificial mounds, many in the form of animals. Excavations there have yielded numbers of tobacco pipes, many with images of animals and some with human heads, in realistic style. Some carvings on shell also show figures of warriors and gods, wearing winged costumes and displaying patterns of face paint. The outline drawings are graceful and convey a sense of activity. No doubt these reflect a warrior-dominated society and some of the figures carry heads as if they were highly prized trophies.

Moving down to South America, the great art work of the village-dwelling Indians who live in the Amazonian rain forests is primarily concerned with personal ornament of various kinds such as painting of face and body, and beautiful ornaments made of feathers and beetles' wing-cases. In these societies there is rarely any special costume for the chief, but as he is responsible for arranging ceremonies he has considerable influence on the total artistic impression.

This is also true of the North American tribes of the Great Plains. Here the civil chief wore a special feathered headdress; he appointed a war chief to conduct raids and organize defense tactics. There was a special long-tailed war bonnet for

A 19th century Navajo blanket represents a 'sand painting' ceremony. The outer frame of the scene shows the Changing Woman, who gave maize to the Navajo. The maize plant stands in the centre.

such men. Each man was aided by his wife, who made his clothing splendid with embroideries of dyed porcupine quills to show his importance.

Each warrior of these tribes possessed a bison-skin wrap on which he painted scenes from his personal history. These painted stories had great influence in the selection of a man as a chief, since they depicted the truth in the eyes of his neighbours. A false entry was punished by humiliating jokes. A few elders kept a record of events on bison skins; each year was marked by a symbolic picture of a famous event of the year. These Plains Indians were planters as well as hunters, but agricultural themes hardly appear in their crafts.

In the southwest of the North American continent, and also in northern Argentina, tribes built themselves houses of stone blocks and made pottery which was painted with geometrical designs. The Pueblo Indians of North America made splendid blankets, and painted ceremonial wooden objects to bring luck. Model figures of fertility spirits, called *kachinas*, were painted in colour. Walls of houses were frescoed with sacred paintings. There was a recognition of artistic quality: the wares made by famous women potters were sought after within the community, as they are today by collectors. In olden times, the Navajo hunted near the Pueblos; their sand paintings and blankets were made in Pueblo styles, but gradually evolved into splendid original works.

Mexico was the home of many civilizations before the arrival of the Spaniards. The earlier periods seem to have been under the domination of priest-kings and the art was inspired primarily by religious belief. The images of the gods and calendric symbols of the passage of time were important for magical purposes.

In the later periods of Toltec and Aztec rule, there was a development of arts linked with the warrior cults. The architectural arts were developed to the point where multi-roomed palaces with painted walls were constructed, and splendid temple buildings were placed on top of huge pyramidal structures. These were covered with sculptures of monumental size, which were coated with limewash and painted in brilliant colours.

Special sculptures and wood carvings were prepared for the nobility and magnificent garments were woven. Fine shields and fans of featherwork were important in this social group. Parallel with the nobility were the priests, who commanded the services of many professional artists, mostly sculptors and painters. Only in the latest period was there any attempt at realism; mostly the forms were symbolic. Pottery for the nobility and for the temples was brilliantly painted; for the common people it was

Photoresources/Royal Scottish Museum Edinburgh

The Indians of Northwest America have been (and still are) particularly prolific wood-carvers. This brightly painted shaman's rattle represents the mythical Thunderbird, believed to create thunder and lightning.

well made but painted with black linear designs only.

Bands of traders brought in turquoise from the Pueblos to the north, jade from Guatemala and gold from Costa Rica. The working of gold for jewellery reached Mexico only in the 8th century AD. Jade was used for precious ornaments and for sculptures, such as the figure of Quetzalcoatl, made in 1508 and now in the British Museum.

To the south of the early Mexicans were the Maya, whose work in the 3rd to 10th centuries included the preparation of stucco reliefs and the carving of great stone pillars to mark the passing of time. Maya society was dominated by its priests, and the Maya arts were mostly dedicated to religion in the form of images of the gods. Both Maya and Mexicans possessed books consisting of long strips, folded in a zig-zag pattern. They were painted on long strips of prepared deer skin, or on cloth made of bark. The Mexicans used a direct pictorial approach, something like a modern comic strip without words. The Maya writing using about 850 symbols representing syllables, the only example of phonetic writing in ancient America.

From the south of Mexico to the Isthmus of Panama there were many small tribes, all ruled by chiefs who used much gold for ornament. Pearls were used to decorate the persons of nobles, and divine images. The high points of local art styles are mostly in painted pottery, though in Costa Rica much effort was expended in making richly designed stone stools to sit on while grinding maize.

Further south in Columbia similar patterns prevailed: local chieftains ruled small tribes with fine artistic skills. From the Cauca River Valley come great quantities of well modelled gold work, much of it very skilfully alloyed with copper. The high point of this art was among the cannibalistic Quimbaya people, who made near-realistic figures of their nobles in gold, highly burnished and expressing a strange cruelty. In the Colombian highlands, modelled plaques of gold were made which present scenes of Chibcha court life in vertical flat figures set on a metal plate. From the east of the Andes there are great human-dragon figures from an early civilization around San Augustin.

Gold was important in all the cultures of the Andes mountain-range of South America. It first appears on the Peruvian coast around 900 BC and later in the mountains around Chavin. In all subsequent Peruvian cultures, gold, copper and silver were extensively used.

Peru was the most highly organized society in all the Americas. The people were ruled by powerful chiefs, until eventually the Inca from Cuzco appropriated all gold for the service of the Sun God and his child, the Supreme Inca. This divine king ruled the land according to surprisingly modern political principles; there was a total welfare organization, paid for with tributes of goods which were kept for distribution in times of need. Hence the highly organized workshops produced great quantities of ceramics and textiles for the royal and divine stores.

The Inca styles were different from those of earlier cultures; they are more strictly graded. Patterns on clothing and pottery show a gradation of complexity according to social levels. Each tribe subject to the Incas had to wear a distinctive identifying costume. Thus the arts were kept under strict control, losing some individuality and liveliness, but their technical quality was superb.

Burial sites in the sands of the Peruvian coastal desert have yielded quantities of magnificent textiles. The most elaborate were woven in communal workshops for the nobility of the coastal states; every type of weaving known to modern people was done on simple hand looms.

Pottery was also beautifully made. An unusual feature is the presence of realistic portrait vases, from the 3rd to the 6th centuries AD. In pyramids and temples the walls were frescoed with designs similar to those on the pottery and textiles. It is clear that this work was done by specialist technicians for a powerful ruling class. There was also a great deal of fine wood carving, but little of it has survived.

Masters of gold and silver, the Peruvians also made tools and weapons of bronze. From stone they made great bowls and, in their later history, they built palaces and temples of finely worked stone, sometimes with figures of serpents and llamas in relief. Even the hardest rocks were used and worked with great patience.

Eventually the Americas were colonized by Spanish, French and British settlers. The Indians were taught new kinds of art, and many of them made beautiful things in the new styles. However, their own arts did not die out altogether. The Eskimo have learned to make stone sculpture and lithographs which are sold in art galleries all over the world. The Pueblo Indians are skilled at pottery and silver work, while their Navajo neighbours make silver and turquoise jewellery and weave fine blankets. In Mexico the Indians make jewellery and toys for the tourists, while in South America there is a trade in silver work from the Indians of Chile. In the forests the remaining Indians still make excellent basket work and beautiful feather decorations.

There has been (and still is) much hardship among the Indians, but they remain proud of their ancestry, and in some places have revived their ancestral arts. In British Colombia weaving blankets and carving totem poles has had an astonishing revival. Many of the Plains Indians have become well-known painters, using traditional themes on their canvases. Though the Amerindian artists are working in a totally different environment, they retain the urge to create. □

Moslem Art

The art of Islam embraces a society which reached from Spain and the Balkans through Turkey, Persia, Arabia, Central Asia, and India to Indonesia. It also extended round the Mediterranean coast and penetrated deeply into Africa.

The unifying link of these varied regions was the religion of Islam, preached by the Prophet Mohammed in the 7th century AD and carried by the Arabs, as they conquered the Middle East only a few decades after the Prophet's death. Within the framework of this monotheistic faith there developed an art of great vitality—with parallel strains of abstraction and representation enriched by regional diversity.

The media through which Islamic art is expressed are extensive: architecture—both religious and secular—ceramics, glass, metalwork, wood, ivory, paintings, calligraphy, textiles and carpets. Only sculpture in the round and large-scale easel painting were not developed as in the West, though a remarkable group of large oil paintings were painted in Persia during the 18th and 19th centuries. By this time, because of increasing political and economic involvement, many Western influences had permeated the tradition of Islamic art.

Art often reflects the major preoccupations of a society. Islamic art does not differ from Christian art in this respect since it emphasizes religion. The greatest buildings, the mosques, are devoted to religion while the creations of the applied or decorative arts embellish them. Among numerous examples are the enamelled glass mosque lamps of Syria, the brilliant panels of glazed ceramic tiles of Persia and Turkey, metalwork candlesticks, wooden Koran stands and pulpits, the carpets lining the spacious interiors of Turkish mosques, and the application of the best calligraphy to Korans.

The art of Islam is basically a synthesis of the artistic traditions of the many peoples who were incorporated in the Moslem state. Its individuality derives from the way in which elements from such traditions were selected and blended. Although many questions can still be asked about the origins of Islamic art, the main line is clear. The Arabs coming from a barren desert environment brought no highly developed art forms with them to their conquered territories, and therefore had to borrow from their subject peoples. At times 'borrowing' meant 'occupation'; for example the Umayyad Mosque in Damascus dated 705–715 was built into the remains of a Roman temple and decorated with mosaic panels of landscape scenes. Curiously this habit recurred long after the need for it had disappeared: the Ottoman Turks in their conquest of Greece in the 15th and 16th centuries converted Orthodox churches, in addition to building mosques.

Generally speaking two main streams

The forms used in Moslem art often reflected religious uses, as in this 16th century lamp from the Sulimaniyeh Mosque in Istanbul.

Michael Holford/V. & A.

of influence contribute to the formation of Islamic art. Firstly the late Graeco-Roman tradition found in Byzantium, Syria, Palestine and Egypt was based on the naturalistic observation of plant and animal life. The coiling vine or ivy was a favourite motif in this tradition. Secondly the Eastern tradition of Sassanian Persia with its links with Central Asia was a stylized art of repeating symmetrical patterns which also favoured palmettes, rosettes, and fantasy motifs such as griffins and winged lions. Several striking examples of the fusion of these traditions may be cited. The 8th century palace of Khirbet al Majfar in Jordan is decorated with stucco patterns in which acanthus rosettes and grapevines of late Graeco-Roman tradition are combined with figures showing Central Asian features. The Friday Mosque at Nain in Persia, of about 960 AD, was built to the plan of an open court with deep colonnaded bays along the side facing Mecca—a plan which came to be standard in parts of the Moslem world—but the stucco decoration of its thick pillars reproduces scrolling vines derived from the classical repertoire.

Three very distinctive features which may be described as characteristic of Islamic art emerged out of the crucible—a feeling for continuous and often abstract pattern, the arabesque motif and the use of calligraphy. The interest in continuous patterns harmonizes well with a passion for surface decoration. Infinitely repeating geometrical designs based on interlocking forms give the effect of dissolving the structure of the objects they decorate.

Arabesque motifs and calligraphy can also be adapted to the requirements of the continuous surface. The arabesque is a stylized plant scroll pattern developed from the classical vine, whose components of stem, leaf and tendril can be extended indefinitely, thus producing a design motif perfect in its adaptability to any media. Such a motif can be shaped to twine around a mosque dome as in the colourful tile mosaic arabesques in the domes of the 17th century Royal Mosque and Sheikh Lotfallah Mosque at Isfahan. It can also be used as a flowering border on pottery, as an ornamental device on a manuscript page or as a repeating medallion in metalwork and carpets.

Calligraphy, the art of elegant writing, was esteemed in the Moslem world far more than in the West, and the calligrapher held an honoured place in society, especially as the language of the Koran—God's revealed word—was Arabic. The script in which this language was written therefore was equally respected. Not only Arabic but also the Persian, Ottoman Turkish and Malay languages used it; the skill of calligraphers was not confined to religion, as secular manuscripts were also beautifully written. The Arabic script possesses powerful decorative attributes; as a cursive script running from right to left with emphasis on the vertical strokes, it formed a naturally rhythmic motif which could be adapted to all surfaces and shapes.

Various styles developed based on two main scripts—angular Kufic and cursive Nashki. Kufic, one of the earliest scripts, stresses the vertical strokes and angular shapes of the letters. It is seen at its purest in Koran manuscripts of the 8th to 9th centuries, where it is written in stark shapes on parchment, though it also occurs as ornamentation on pottery, textiles and architecture. Among the numerous variations of Kufic which developed, one of the most striking is the so-called floriate Kufic, in which the vertical strokes are made more exuberant by terminating them in floral motifs and scrolls. From the 11th century the Nashki style became more popular. It is less austere than Kufic and has boldly curved letters; an especially beautiful variant called *thuluth* was suited for deep bands of inscription, which were used to great effect especially around metal candlesticks and enamelled glass mosque lamps.

There were endless variations on the use of calligraphy. The Ottoman Turks delighted in devices such as birds and animals made out of the letters of inscription, and also developed the beautiful *tughras* or signatures of the Sultan, where the letters were spread out like a stylized hand. Different styles of calligraphy were used together to great effect. A 15th century religious complex at Natanz in Persia has its portal decorated with a band of geometric Kufic running parallel with a band of *nast'aliq*, a graceful and fluent script developed in Persia.

It is commonly and mistakenly supposed that Islam forbids the representation of images—human or animal—and that consequently all Islamic art is abstract. This is incorrect, as the Koran does not mention any prohibition and the abundant surviving examples of pictorial art contradict any such theory. Generally, however, figural imagery was discouraged in religious art, which explains why the decoration of mosques and related buildings is non-representational, and exploits instead the full repertoire of calligraphy and geometrical pattern. There is also no didactic tradition, as there is in Christian art, of using painting to depict religious themes for the benefit of the illiterate. Certain exceptions exist, such as a series of 16th century Turkish miniature paintings illustrating the biography of the Prophet Mohammed—who is represented veiled and enveloped in a halo of flames. On a more popular level, religious prints in Persia show the tragic events leading to the martyrdom of the Imam Hussein, one of the most revered figures of the Shi'a sect of Islam.

While realism in the European sense of copying from life models does not occur in Islamic art, there is nonetheless a lively pictorial tradition in which life situations are used. Islamic society is seen as the Moslem artist wanted it to be seen; for example, subjects chosen from the stories of Persian and Arabic literature and folklore reflect mental and emotional attitudes, while the scenes of the hunting field, market place and so forth, show the essential features of contemporary life through the painter's conventions.

Islamic art is well suited to the needs of its society while admirably combining beauty with function. This is strikingly apparent in architecture, one of its greatest achievements. Early Moslem worship took place either in an open enclosure or in converted buildings, but a distinctive place of worship—the mosque —developed with features of its own. The

The nomadic background of many Moslem peoples is reflected in houses containing little formal furniture. Mattresses and cushions could be used for both sitting and sleeping and were covered with beautiful pile carpets.

Islamic art inherited and transmitted Greek culture and science and in the process made many advances. This 14th century Istanbul manuscript summarized existing knowledge about the use and health of horses.

Michael Holford/V. & A.

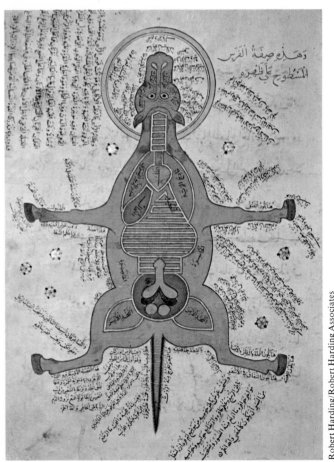
Robert Harding/Robert Harding Associates

basic liturgical requirements of Islam are simple, reflecting the desert origin of the faith. Divine service consists essentially of prayer and needs no special objects or vestments for its celebration. The so-called *qibla* wall with a niche or *mihrab* facing towards Mecca indicates the direction of prayer; an enclosure is needed sufficient to house the worshippers; a tower or minaret enables the *muezzin* to call the faithful to prayer; and a *mimbar* or pulpit is required for the prayer leader. Using these elements an impressive architecture developed according to variations of local environment, available materials and existing craft traditions.

Thus the earliest building specifically constructed as a mosque, the Dome of the Rock built in 691 AD at Jerusalem, structurally and decoratively owes much to Byzantine tradition.

The mosque of Ibn Tulun in Cairo of 876–879 AD, is built on what is known as the colonnaded mosque plan or the classic Arab plan. It is built of brick, an easily obtainable building material in Egypt, and has colonnades round an open court; the side with the *mihrab* has multiple rows of columns forming a deep hall. Such a plan is brilliantly elaborated in the Great Mosque of Cordoba of 10th century date, where the Islamic love of surface decoration is also seen in luxuriant carved and moulded stucco patterns applied over the brick.

Mosques in Persia were built of brick, the most conveniently available building material, and were based on the square or rectangular open-court plan, feasible in a hot climate. Certain elements were incorporated from pre-Islamic Sassanian architecture such as the *iwan*—a large vaulted hall open on one side. An *iwan* is situated in the centre of each side of the Persian mosque and can be developed according to its function; for example, the *iwan* at the entrance is elaborated into a high portal, while the *iwan* before the prayer niche or *mihrab* leads into a domed chamber.

Other Sassanian devices used in a Persian mosque are technical, such as the squinch which is an arch slung across each corner of a square chamber to allow a transition to a hemispherical dome. The open court punctuated by *iwans* was to be the classic plan of the Persian mosque from the 11th through to the 19th century upon which dazzling variations in decoration were wrought. These range from austere Seljuk structures of the 11th–12th centuries, which relied for effect on brick masonry relieved by magnificently worked stucco, to the luminous creations of 17th century Isfahan, in which structure is less visually important than the wealth of tilework decoration in predominant tones of blue and turquoise, which incorporates all the repertoire of Islamic design.

S. H. Zaidi/Robert Harding Associates

Islamic painting was most elaborately developed at the courts of the Moghuls in India. In this 18th century miniature, the famous emperor Shah Jehan and his four sons are listening to a holy man.

The open court plan of the Persian mosque with its four *iwans* was versatile and could be extended to other structures. The *Madresseh*, or religious college, was built to the same plan. Here in addition to the *iwan* and domed sanctuary chamber, the remaining *iwans* conveniently served as lecture halls, while the arches of the arcaded sides opened into rooms for the accommodation of students. The open-court plan could also be adapted for secular use as is shown by the *caravansarai*—a large roadside inn. The walls offered a sheltered enclosure for both travellers and baggage animals.

Accommodation of varying degrees was provided; suites of rooms were built into the *iwans* to make comfortable quarters for rich guests, while the side walls were divided into rooms for ordinary travellers. The similarity in structure is also paralleled by the close administrative connection between religious and secular buildings as revenues from a *caravansarai* were often used to finance a mosque or *madresseh*.

In contrast to Persia are the solutions found by the architects of Ottoman Turkey, where climatic conditions made the open-court mosque impractical, and stone was in abundant supply as a building material. The Byzantines had already explored the use of stone and had constructed large churches using domes and semidomes. The Ottomans adopted the

A 14th century glazed tile from the wall of a mosque at Khonsar, Iran.

Michael Holford/V. & A.

for lamps and vessels. In secular architecture the relation is similarly intimate.

Moslem households of traditional type had neither furniture nor a rigid functional division of rooms. Floors were covered with pile-woven carpets in silk or wool, which is one of the textile arts most associated with the Islamic world. Carpets were woven in a range of virtuoso designs—floral patterns and vivid pictorial scenes being favoured in Persia and Moghul India, while more formal and geometrical motifs were used in Turkey and Egypt. Rooms could easily be converted into dining rooms by laying a cloth on the carpet, into bedrooms by bringing out quilts and pillows and into

A 13th century Persian bowl with underglaze decoration.

Michael Holford/V. & A.

same techniques—and indeed converted churches to use as mosques. But they made considerable advances and Ottoman mosques are built of beautifully worked stone masonry—usually a silver-grey limestone—and constructed in the form of a domed cube on which astonishing geometrical variations were wrought.

The ultimate achievements here can be seen in the great mosques of Istanbul constructed during the 16th and 17th centuries in which every experiment was tried in enclosing a huge volume within a cascade of tightly related domes and semidomes interrupted by the forcefulness of rocket-like minarets. Unembellished, these mosques rely on structure rather than decoration for effect.

Interiors, however, could be lavish—adorned with sumptuous ceramic tile panels, painted arabesques and inscriptions inside domes and with soft carpets. In contrast to the styles developed in sophisticated cultures the mosques of the Persian Gulf region were simple constructions of coral blocks held together by lime mortar.

Comparatively little secular architecture survives, as it was built less solidly than the great religious monuments. (The situation is comparable in Europe, where great medieval cathedrals survive, but little or nothing of the houses surrounding them.) Like religious architecture, however, secular architecture was well adapted to local conditions.

In Persia, with its dusty climate, houses were constructed with thick brick walls for coolness. All attention was concentrated on the interior, which in traditional households was centred round a courtyard often made into an inviting refuge from the outside world by the inclusion of ornamental ponds, channels of running water, flowers and trees. Large windows gave access to this courtyard from the room. Islam's decorative arts are intimately linked to the embellishment of architecture; for example, in religious architecture there is lavish use of ceramic tiles in Persian and Turkish mosques, while glass and metal are used

The great mosque built by Ibn Tulun in Cairo uses a local material, brick, covered with stucco. The decoration derives from earlier styles but is used to give the building a definitely Islamic character.

Andrew Baring

reception rooms by bringing in cushions for host and guests to recline on. Precious objects, utensils and books were kept in niches recessed into the walls while supplies of bedding and clothes were kept in chests.

Ceramics were used both for everyday utensils and for luxury objects in which a high degree of technical excellence was reached. Many decorative methods were explored such as slip-painting, *sgraffiato* (where designs were incised through a thick clay slip), and underglaze painting. From the many fine wares, lustre-painted pottery must be singled out as one of the most distinctive products of Islamic ceramics. The finest lustre wares are associated with Iraq of the 9th–10th centuries, Egypt of the 10th–12th centuries and Persia of the 12th–14th centuries. For lustre painting the vessel was

made out of fine clay and usually glazed white—though sometimes as in Persia a blue or turquoise glaze was used—and fired. Then it was painted with flowing designs—scrolls, arabesques, human and animal figure scenes, and inscriptions, in pigments which when fired again produced a golden lustre. This technique was also used for tiles, but more usually tiles were made by the techniques of overglaze and underglaze polychrome painting; the brilliant tiles of Persia and Turkey were created by these methods.

The metalworker's craft was widely practised in Islamic society using the same techniques which are still seen in the Middle Eastern bazaar today. A wide range of objects for religious and secular use were made—boxes, candlesticks, bowls, basins, jugs, incense burners. As in ceramics they were distinguished by a special technique—the predominant use of bronze or brass with the design inlaid in silver and gold, thus achieving a dramatic contrast between the sombre background metal and the lustre of the decoration. The designs of metalwork were made up of the common repertoire of arabesque, inscription and figure scene. Often the figure scenes were treated with a suppleness which recalls painting.

Islamic painting was principally a luxury art devoted to manuscript illustration. It is here that royal and wealthy patronage exerted a great influence; thus the Shahs of Persia, the Sultans of Ottoman Turkey, and the rulers of Moghul India all encouraged distinctive styles of painting. Though many styles developed they all share the common qualities of brilliant colour, meticulous detail in their rendering of a scene, and a formal treatment of composition and atmosphere in which all objects are equally illuminated. Within these conventions it was possible to depict an enormous range of themes, from the fantasy of the legends associated with the Prophet Mohammed's ascent to heaven, through the dazzling court scenes of Persia and Moghul India, to the lively representation of traditional festivals and the Ottoman sultans campaigns. □

The Art of West Coastal Africa

It is an interesting fact that most of the African works of art to be seen today in Western museums and private collections come from western Africa, south of the great Niger-Benue river complex and west of the Great Lakes which divide the Congo Basin from East Africa. Although the distribution of artefacts in museums is partly the result of arbitrary decisions in the course of the formation of the collections, the consistency of the pattern is remarkable and says something important about the nature of African Art.

The people inhabiting this area of western Africa show considerable physical similarity. They are, in effect, the true Negroes and are little mixed with other peoples. This is mainly because malaria is widespread in the coastal forest area and peoples with no hereditary resistance to the disease found it difficult to survive there before the 20th century. While peoples in the savannah to the north mixed first with Berbers and then Arabs, the coastal forest-dwellers were more isolated. Nilotes and Cushites from Ethiopia mixed with the Negroes in the east, and in the south the Bushmen peoples were largely absorbed by them—but the art in these regions is much less significant.

Although there may possibly be an hereditary predisposition to artistic creativity, the most satisfactory explanation of this distribution is cultural. And since the most powerful vehicle of culture is language, it is worth looking at the distribution of languages within the region. This gives a clear indication of the region's cultural homogeneity—all the languages belong to the same Niger-Congo family.

And there are other cultural similarities. The societies of the forest tend to be small scale, often without powerful rulers or elaborate states. In the course of history this has sometimes changed, but it is generally true. Where social order and cohesion are not maintained by a strong central 'government', different techniques have been developed, in which other features of social organization, like the family, the clan and the secret society, are employed. All are backed up by religious beliefs and both social and economic sanctions.

The result is a closely integrated society in which many forces tend to the same

(Above right) Between 500 BC and 200 AD, farmers on the Jos Plateau in Nigeria made sophisticated and forceful terracotta heads which have been found at Nok.

(Above left) Egyptian art stems from the same sources as Negro art. Animals like this ram from Karnak feature in both religious traditions.

(Bottom) Civilization in Napata-Meroe in the Sudan owed much to Ancient Egypt. But the naturalism of some of its art, like this king's head, is more African than Mediterranean.

end. Worship of the ancestors, for example, is a religious, social and family duty. It relates to ideas of cosmic as well as social order, and is a vehicle for the control of psychological and spiritual forces. In much of Africa the universe is seen as controlled by these forces; causes are seen as personal, and natural effects are the results of an exercise of will—either by a human being or by a spirit or god. The mechanistic conception of the world, and its ordering in terms of forces like 'gravity', is Western, not part of most traditional African beliefs.

It is a prime purpose of much African art to help society control these powerful forces. The relationship of the individual

to his family and his ancestors, the relationship of a group to the whole society, and of the whole society to the land, all involve proper adjustments which are effected by ritual. Masks and carved figures become actors and play an important part in this process by personalizing the forces being manipulated and by dramatizing their relationship It works

(Left) Ife culture advanced techniques used at Nok to make terra-cotta heads, and further extended them to bronze-casting. This royal head shows similarities in style and ornamentation to the art of Meroe.

This gazelle mask from the Guro tribe of Ivory Coast is part of a costume worn during the initiation rituals of the 'Zamble' society.

Werner Forman Archives

Werner Forman Archives

British Museum/Michael Holford

in the same way, whether the 'force' appears abstract, (like 'fertility' or 'increase'), or an animal (like the gazelle, described in Bambara myth as the first teacher of agriculture), or an actual ancestor.

It is because they carry so much real meaning, and because they symbolize so much faith and psychological involvement, that African artefacts have such a powerful effect. They demand fear, respect and understanding. They may be preserved in museums, but they are rarely comparable with other objects found there: they are far more dynamic and vital, and their only true surrounding is in the circumstance where they are used. Understanding them requires more social than aesthetic judgement.

The 'art' region of Western Africa is dominated by the thick tropical rain-forests of the Guinea Coast and the Congo Basin, and the ready availability of wood has clearly been of the greatest importance to the history of African art. Some of the forms adopted—the frequent use of the cylinder, for example, in masks, stools, and figures—derive from the natural shape of the tree. Eccentric roots and branches are sometimes exploited for free-form carvings, of which certain Dogon examples are the most brilliant.

The forest also provides different kinds of wood with different characteristics suited to a variety of purposes. There are hard and strong woods, ideal for building, which are difficult to carve but which last a long time. The many soft-woods, on the other hand, offer the artist a tractable material for more detailed carving. Some woods are heavy, and are used for making figures for display or for the kinds of

(Left) Ivory carvings like this salt-cellar were once found in royal collections in Europe. Commissioned by the Portuguese, they are related in style to soapstone 'nomoli' figures from Sierra Leone.

Werner Forman Archives

possible that bone and ivory were used for works of art from early times, but no important early carvings in these materials have been found outside Ancient Egypt. The oldest ivory objects from western Africa are the brilliantly carved salt-cellars brought back by the Portuguese shortly after they discovered the coast at the end of the 15th century. Their form reflects existing styles and shows considerable similarity to the *nomoli* figures carved from soapstone by the Sherbro peoples of Sierra Leone. This is only one example of the way in which African art absorbs foreign influences but produces objects of a very African character. There are perhaps 70 or 80 Afro-Portuguese ivories in existence and they are a remarkable example of cultural co-operation.

Elephants do not generally live in heavy forests and are most common where it gives way to the savannah; the peoples who have made the best use of ivory are mostly found near these points. The most famous examples come from Benin in Nigeria—the magnificent pairs of lions, with copper pots, and the pectoral masks are among the most splendid works of

Most Dogon sculpture is in the spare, abstract style common in the Niger Bend region. Powerful figures like this horse and rider express the Dogon obsession with their rich and complex mythology.

The court of the King of Asanti exploited local gold resources in a spectacular manner. It was used for jewellery and ornaments like the decorations on this royal cap.

ceremonial use where strength is important. The 'pestle-statues' of the Senufo, for example, are beaten on the ground by initiates of the *Lo* society to induce fertility. Lightweight woods are more suitable where a mask, often of considerable size and elaboration, has to be worn in a ritual dance.

The forest also supplies seeds and vegetable dyes for decoration: the Bapende and the Bakuba peoples of Zaire, for example, make extensive use of powdered camwood to colour their carvings. Palm oil is frequently used to give colour, shine and protection to wooden artefacts. The great potential of the forest accounts for much of the variety in African art; conversely, the overall similarity of the environment, even though it is occupied by many different peoples, contributes to the unity of social and religious philosophy which inspires that art.

Other materials are used in African art, but in the face of the overwhelming preponderance of wood, they look like intrusions (which—in both historical and technical terms—they are). It is

Michael Holford

art in the world. More intimate, and very appealing, are the ivory neck-rests of the Baluba from southeastern Zaire.

But Africans have mostly used ivory as an export commodity, and even where they carve it, as they do now in some quantity, it is mostly with the tourist in mind. The main indigenous use has been in jewellery like armlets or for knife-handles. This is a craft rather than 'art' use in Western terms, but the distinction is not one Africans traditionally make.

Stone has been used in African art, but technical limitations have combined with the conservative attachment to wood

Beadwork is often used for decoration in Nigeria and Cameroun. This example is from the jacket of a figure of Eshu, the Yoruba deity who acts as a messenger between the gods and mankind.

The Yoruba of western Nigeria and Dahomey are among the most skilled wood-carvers in Africa. This Egungun mask is one of many kinds worn in honour of the gods.

British Museum/Michael Holford

Werner Forman Archives

to restrict its use. The Sherbro *nomoli* have been mentioned: they are similar to the *pomtan* figures of the neighbouring Kissi. Phallic columns of stone are found in several places. There are many in southwestern Ethiopia among the Sidamo peoples, a few in the Sudan, and perhaps as many as 300 in southeastern Nigeria.

The last group are carefully carved and range from a comparatively plain phallus shape to a more elaborate human form, where the glans is treated as the 'head' and the 'body' is carved in shallow relief to indicate arms and scarification; the navel is accentuated. Many of the columns are named after former village headmen and sacrifices with ancestral and fertility connotations are performed at these sites. The stone carvings of the Bankongo, who live in the area around the mouth of the Congo River, commemorate the people's ancient kings.

In some ways terracotta is akin to stone: it is hard, it can take detail and it is difficult to destroy. It is possible that its use in West Africa was influenced by stone. On the Jos Plateau in Nigeria a number of the most extraordinary terracotta heads have been found, which show great mastery of the medium and have a

most powerful impact. Dated by the Carbon-14 method to between 500 BC and 200 AD, they are the earliest important West African artefacts. Stylistic and technical affinities indicate that the terracotta heads of Ife, the spiritual 'centre' of the Yoruba people, carried on this tradition 1,000 years later.

The rounded forms of the Ife heads are more obviously naturalistic than the earlier ones (called Nok, after an important site where some were found). It is interesting that one Ife terracotta has been found representing the head of a ram. It is very similar to heads of the ram-god Amun from Ancient Egypt. But like the Nok heads, most of the Ife heads are of humans, presumably of rulers. And it is tempting to suggest that the similarity these show to some stone carvings from Meroe in the Sudan indicates a combination of this style with the terracotta technique. Several features in

The great pillars of the Oba's palace at Benin were covered with bronze plaques cast in relief. This one shows the sacrifice of a bull which the Oba performed each year at his father's shrine.

the headdress of Ife heads are reminiscent of Meroe, while the Yoruba themselves have a tradition that they came to Nigeria from the northeast. Meroe was destroyed by Axum, then the capital of an Ethiopian empire, in the mid-14th century AD. Although it owed much to Ancient Egypt, Meroe had always been a very African state, and perhaps its rulers escaped to a sympathetic home in the west. The end of

the Nok culture and the beginning of the Yoruba would thus be explicable by a migration from the east.

Another technical innovation which may have come by the same route is bronze-casting. The earliest bronzes found in Nigeria were probably made at Idah on the confluence of the Niger and the Benue. In the late 15th century a group of these bronzes was taken to Nupeland

on the Niger further west. This 'Tsoede' group, found at Jebba and Tada, contains the largest bronzes found in Africa. They are works of original, and considerable, inspiration: most famous are the standing bowman from Jebba and the seated male figure from Tada. It is not known when the Yoruba of Ife first turned from terracotta to bronze, but the stylistic continuity between the two

media is clear. Some bronzes have scarification all over the face and head-dresses exactly similar to the terracottas. All are marked by the same refined and idealized realism.

Tradition has it that the knowledge of casting bronze by the 'lost-wax' method passed from Ife to Benin in the 13th century. In Benin it remained a royal monopoly until the 19th century. The king or *Oba* would have heads made of his predecessor and royal shrines would thus contain a whole succession of busts. They mostly have holes in the top to hold carved tusks and were placed on altars at which regular sacrifices were made. Bronze was also used for the square plaques which decorated the pillars of the *Obas*' palaces and courts. The shape may derive from the Portuguese idea of a picture, but the aesthetic is purely African. Many bronzes, royal heads and ivories were carried off by the British after they had attacked Benin City at the end of the 19th century.

Gold is the other metal which has been

The Bakota of Gabon make highly schematized figures covered with brass and copper sheeting. They are placed as guardians over the bones in Kota ancestor shrines.

The Ikoi people of southeastern Nigeria carved a number of phallic shaped stone figures with human faces. These 'Akwanshi' usually bear the names of former village headmen, and sacrifices are made to them to promote the health and prosperity of the villagers.

British Museum/Michael Holford

Werner Forman Archives

important in African art and again it is closely connected with royalty. The people most famous for their gold work are the Asanti of Ghana. They were fortunate that the area they conquered contained considerable resources of gold (which are still exploited today). It was used by kings and princes to decorate their dress and furniture and to make remarkable jewellery. The Asanti mask from the treasure of the *Asantehene* Kofi Kakari—now in the Wallace Collection—possesses an almost ghostly majesty. It may represent a powerful conquered king, for a ring under the chin suggests that it was hung upside-down.

Connected with the exploitation of the metal, bronze was used to make innumerable weights and boxes for storing gold dust. These are decorated with symbolic designs or small figures illustrating legends and proverbs. Later imitations are still

The Bushongo are a sub-tribe of the Bakuba in Zaire, who brought many peoples together to form a strongly centralized kingdom. This small statue represents King Bom Bosh, the 96th Nyimi of Bakuba.

being cast, just as in Benin and in the grasslands of Cameroun the Nigerian tradition survives in a distant and decadent form.

All these arts employing sophisticated techniques are associated with courts and royalty. They are therefore more at home in the marginal areas than in the heart of the forest, but it would be wrong to consider them, as has sometimes been done, as non-African. Even though some elements of technique are imported, both style and function are authentically African. Nevertheless, in purely statistical terms they are 'abnormal': the most basic and consistent forms of African art remain geared to the integrating philosophy of the forest just as their material substance derives from it.

The Negro societies which Europeans first encountered were in the west, but as the Portuguese pursued their discoveries so they advanced eastward to the Congo region. It is useful to follow a similar path along the coast from west to east.

The stone figures of the peoples around the Sherbro, the Bulom and the Kissi, and the stylistic similarities between these and the Afro-Portuguese ivories, have been mentioned. Not far away, in what is now the Republic of Guinea, live the Baga whose great *nimba* masks are an excellent illustration of the Negro concern with 'increase' and the vital forces which animate the world.

The institution of the secret society is widely found in much of Guinea, Sierra Leone, Liberia and Ivory Coast. The *Poro,* as it is called, performs many functions—educating the young, supervising initiation, maintaining law and order—contributing to overall social order in many ways. It has also had a unifying effect on artistic style, although considerable variation remains. The serene and restrained form of many Dan masks, with their simplified naturalism, contrasts strikingly with the alarming apparitions made by the Ngere and related peoples like the Gio of Liberia.

East of these peoples, in Ghana and Ivory Coast, live a group of related peoples called the Akan, who include the Asanti whose gold and gold-weights have been mentioned. Their wood-carving is mainly confined to the production of round-faced flat dolls which girls carry at initiation ceremonies and of magnificent stools with complex geometric decoration. The Baule, who split off from Asanti about 240 years ago, make simplified, rather wistful masks, and another sub-tribe, the Agni are famed for

Werner Forman Archives

the terracotta heads made to represent their ancestors and which are found, often in large numbers in sacred groves.

To the north, in Mali, in the region of the great bend of the Niger River are some of the most interesting peoples in Africa. The Dogon have an elaborate mythology and cosmology in which they have an almost obsessive interest. Figures illustrating mythical themes, or representing the ancestors, are made in a spare,

stripped-down style. William Fagg, an authority on African art, has suggested that this may derive from the overlapping of carving and blacksmithing, as one man is often both smith and carver. The Dogon live beyond the forest and the shortage of large pieces of wood may also have been significant, but the main reason for their spare style is probably their philosophical sense of ordered structure and a fine appreciation of what

Werner Forman Archives

The Bakuba peoples of Zaire developed many decorative arts under the patronage of their kings. This pile cloth is made of raffia and is called Kasai Velvet.

is really essential.

The Bambara, who also live in Mali, are famous for their antelope masks, the *tyiwara*. Myth tells how the antelope taught the Bambara agriculture, and the event is recalled in annual agricultural ceremonies. The neighbouring Senufo 'pestle' figures have been mentioned: they also make forceful masks with a stylized face, often decorated with horns, the *kpelie*. These are usually displayed at funerals and protect the soul of the deceased on its journey to the afterworld.

To the east of the Akan are the Yoruba of Nigeria and Dahomey and the related Fon. The great virtuosity shown in the Ife terracottas and their famous quartz stools is also seen in wood. The Yoruba produce elaborate ceremonial masks—those for the *Gelede* society are remarkable, as are those designed for the *epa* ceremony. *Ibeji* figures are made to commemorate twins, and there are a wide range of other figures in honour of gods like Shango, Ogun, Eshu and Olokun. To the east of the Yoruba are the Bini, whose tribal art has largely been overshadowed by that of the court, and to the east of them the Ibo who make small white-faced masks. Further east still are the Ikoi, whose masks are often covered with skin and have a terrifying appearance: they represent dead members of the *ekpo* society.

In Cameroun, especially in the grasslands around Bamenda, are a number of peoples who make a great variety of carved masks, figures and utensils. Stools for chiefs, decorated with carved leopards or elaborate beadwork, show both

sculptural and decorative virtuosity. On the coast near Duala, intricate canoe prows are carved, while to the southeast in Gabon, live the Fang, who are famous for their masks. Since Fang tradition suggests that their origins are in the east, their art is perhaps the art of the peoples whom they conquered and unified: a favourite subject are the heads used to guard ancestral remains.

Guardianship of the dead is also the purpose of the flat, stylized, almost abstract figures made by the Bokota, the neighbours of the Fang. They are covered with brass and copper sheeting, and placed on top of the containers which hold the skulls and bones of ancestors in special shrines. At the mouth of the Ogowe River a number of tribes, like the Mpongwe and the Bapunu, make white-faced masks distinguished by symmetrically arranged keloids—raised scars—on the forehead and temples.

To the south in the Republics of Congo and Zaire, live a cluster of peoples brought together under the domination of the Kongo before the arrival of the Portuguese. It was a highly centralized state and much of its art is designed for the court, like the royal stone and wood figures. The Bakongo also made fetishes, whose power derived from the nails, horns or mirrors which were attached to them. The *moganga* fetishes were for protection, but the *konde* were offensive. Both reflect a widespread western African belief in the efficacy of 'medicines' or magical substances.

Many peoples to the south and east of the Kongo were influenced by them and by their artistic styles, even after the empire began to break up in the 16th century. As part of this process, the Bapende, who specialize in dance masks for initiation ceremonies, moved eastwards where they came under the influence

of another imperialist people, the Lunda.

Between the Bakongo and the Lunda are the Bakuba, whose artefacts are often coloured red, since this colour is the epitome of beauty in their eyes. Their royal statues are famous, as are the beautifully decorated boxes and similar gifts which are given to mourners at the funerals of important people. The decoration often consists of a number of formal, named elements. These designs are applied to utilitarian objects, figures, masks and raffia-cloth and they are even incorporated in the pattern of scarification on the body. Far to the northeast the Zande of the Nile-Congo watershed and the Konso of Ethiopia both carve rather formal standing figures. In both cases they represent ancestors: the Konso figures may also include victims killed and castrated by a famous warrior.

Although there are isolated examples of artistic activity from east and south Africa, there is little to compare with the important works from western Africa. The only possible exception are the Makonde of the Tanzania-Mozambique border, who carve helmet masks imitating the facial scarifications of their wearers. Unfortunately their technical virtuosity has been turned to the production of twisted monstrosities for the tourist trade: an apt illustration of the psychological turmoil which contact with the West has brought to Africa. This contact has brought to an end much of the reason for creating the old magnificent works of art, since it has altered social realities beyond recognition.

Such a brief survey cannot do justice to the immense variety of art which western Africa has produced. But it does illustrate the general point already made, that the reason for this production is both social and spiritual. Ancestors, gods, spirits and other beings are seen as powerful, and involved in a constant relationship with their human brothers, so it is natural that the artistic expression of this should generate considerable intensity.

It is this intensity which is the hallmark of African art. Everything—form, tactile quality, colour and decoration—contributes to heighten intensity. It expresses the total integration of the individual and his family with the larger social group, and the relationship of the group with the spirits. African art merges the present in the past and ties together the whole cosmos. This is why it is so strong, and why it can speak across the vast cultural and technical gulf between the Africa which produced it and the Western technology which threatens to destroy it. In recent years, however, numerous African nations have realized the unique value of their people's art and have begun to take steps to preserve it for future generations. □

Oceanic Art

As an entity with a common tradition or style, Oceanic art does not exist. Oceania has produced a large number of styles in different media, using different materials during different periods. Techniques, styles and attitudes have been developing over a long period of time, making a historical perspective of vital importance for our understanding. But Oceanic societies were not studied by Europeans until the late 18th century and much information about the arts has been lost.

Recent field studies of the visual arts of Melanesia and of music and dance throughout Oceania have yielded insights into the role of art in these societies. These reveal a fundamental difference between the attitudes towards art held by Oceanic people and those generally held by Western societies, where the concept of aesthetics is dominant. Much Western art is created as a result of individual inspiration, but Oceanic art is the product of particular social contexts, created specifically to communicate meaning.

Through the use of symbols, particular shapes, designs, colours, materials or movements, the arts of Oceania gave visual and oral form to beliefs concerning humanity's place within society and the relationship between humans and the supernatural. The creation and display of art was an integral part of social and religious life, and there was usually no rigid distinction between the natural and the supernatural. Aesthetics had their place in the arts of Oceania, but how well an art form conveyed its meaning was considered more important than the subtlety with which materials or colours were used.

The Aborigines, who have inhabited Australia for over 30,000, years were (and still are) a hunting and gathering people who travelled in small bands for most of the year and met as tribal units only on occasions of communal ceremony. Their visual and oral arts are closely connected with beliefs concerning origins and the influences of the supernatural. The world was inhabited by a variety of spirits who, in a historical 'dreamtime' or 'dreaming', were responsible for the creation of the Australian landscape and everything in it. Humans were held to be closely linked to particular spirits of animals, plants or places, the form of which was determined by a number of factors, including conception, birth and parentage.

Striking among Aboriginal visual arts are the painted memorial posts and figures erected by the inhabitants of Arnhem Land and Melville Island, which

Aborigine art reflects their elaborate cosmology. This rock painting from SE Cape York, Australia shows a Quinkan Spirit Being.

Courtesy of Peter Gathercole

The face of an ancestor—a powerful warrior or a famous chief—was carved on this plank which lined the inside of a Maori tribal meeting house.

social organisation and religion.

Figures, masks and carvings were directly related to beliefs concerning spirits, notably ancestor spirits of the recent dead who still influenced earthly affairs and therefore needed to be propitiated. Various animal forms featured widely in Melanesian art: the use of crocodile and fish motifs was a reflection of beliefs concerning powerful forces in the rivers and sea, which brought benefit to humans if the correct ritual observances were performed.

There was and is an enormous diversity of styles in Melanesia. West Irian, the Indonesian half of New Guinea, is noted for the seated wood skull-receptacle figures from the northeast region. The Asmat peoples of the south are skilled wood-carvers and their designs incorporate human, animal and insect motifs, notably on openwork canoe prows and 'hour-glass' drums.

The peoples of the Sepik River area of Papua New Guinea produced brightly painted long-featured masks and figures and other sacred objects, which became imbued with the presence of spirits on ritual occasions and were carefully stored in men's cult houses. These cult houses were often decorated, as among the Abelam, who painted the sago-spathe frontal section with designs which illustrated myths and symbolized human and spirit relationships.

Paint was a very important material in this area, and often magical substances were termed 'paint'. In the New Guinea Highlands, carving was limited, but dramatic body decoration, enhanced by feather,

British Museum/Photoresources

carried symbolic designs associated with the dead man, his position in the social group and his relationship to the spirit world. Because of the Aborigines' mobile life-style, sculpture was not common, but coloured pigments were used in cave painting, bark painting, body decoration and as decoration on implements and ornaments.

Little is known about the elaborate cave paintings and engravings which depict creatures in human and animal form. These are thought to be associated with the complex Aboriginal cosmology and may also have been connected with increase ceremonies, in which the depiction of animals and plants in the ritual context was believed to guarantee the continuation of the species.

Bark paintings were once used in increase ceremonies, in rituals concerning origins and as accessories to hunting magic; they are now mostly produced for

(Right) Hawaiian sculpture is distinctive for its vigour. This wooden carving, with its aggressive stance, gives the impression of considerable power and emotion.

sale. Ritual body decoration with pigments and sometimes blood and feathers was widespread, and the Arunta of Central Australia created elaborate designs representing the emu and other creatures.

Complex designs were engraved on stone or wood tablets, *churinga*, which acted as aids for memorizing myths and rituals. Music and dance were integral parts of formal ritual, the long hollow drone pipe known as *didjeridu* being a popular musical instrument in northern areas.

Melanesia encompasses New Guinea and the groups of islands stretching southeastwards as far as New Caledonia. The islands are mountainous with abundant vegetation and the indigenous populations were (and many still are), village dwellers living in tribal groups, many with loose political structures led by 'big men'. The art forms are closely bound up with the

British Museum/Michael Holford

(Below) The Malanggan wood carvings of New Ireland, with their elaborate open-work designs, were created as temporary receptacles for ancestral spirits.

British Museum/Michael Holford

Museum für Volkerkunde/Michael Holford

shell and fibre ornaments, reflected the competitive spirit within these 'big men' societies. In the south, the Papuan Gulf area produced engraved and painted shields and bark cloth masks. The Massim region of the southeast peninsula and offshore islands had a distinctive curvilinear carving style, which was used to decorate such objects as canoe prows and shields and was derived from the curving beak, neck and wings of the frigate bird.

The inhabitants of the Bismarck Archipelago were similar in many respects to the peoples of northern New Guinea. Belief in the power of recently dead ancestors was widespread and masks and figures featured strongly in rituals that dramatized these beliefs. Most striking are the *malanggan* carvings of New Ireland, which usually depict a human figure with fish, birds and snakes incorporated into elaborate openwork designs. These were created to act as temporary receptacles for ancestral spirits during memorial and initiation ceremonies, and were subsequently discarded—often into the hands of European collectors who saw permanent aesthetic value in them.

Masquerades were performed during the *malanggan* ceremonial and were important in the rituals of peoples in New Britain, where masks were made from skulls and from large conical structures covered with painted bark cloth.

In the Solomon Islands there were two major style areas: the northwest, where carved and painted designs approximated those of New Britain, and the southeast, where a style was developed using iri-

The peoples of the Sepik River Valley of New Guinea often used human skulls as a basis for decoration. These sacred objects became inspired by spirits on ceremonial occasions.

descent pearl and conus-shell inlay on blackened wood. Solomon Islands' art often included marine elements: fish appears on dance batons, paddles and ornaments, or as individual sculptures displayed during initiation rites for youths, and sea birds were another common motif. Elegant canoes with upswept bow and stern sections were decorated with shell inlay and attachments, and small figures, usually lacking the lower body, were fastened to the bows of canoes, symbolizing a tutelary spirit who protected the canoe from hazards at sea. The variety of dance accessories—shields, batons, paddles and ornaments—indicates the importance of dance in ceremonial.

The art of Vanatua, besides reflecting ideas about the supernatural, is closely linked to the system of social organization based on graded male secret societies. On Malakula Island, figures and masks of wood, clay and cob-web fibres are decorated with bright pigments, while large slit gongs, their upper parts carved as heads, were embedded upright in dancing grounds. The island of Ambrym is noted for large figures carved from fibrous fern trees.

A different system of social stratification operated in New Caledonia, where symbols of authority, notably axes, were made from jade, wood, bark cloth, coconut shell and reddish cordage made from the fur of the flying fox, or fruit bat. Pigments were not widely used and wood masks and figures were normally plain, exhibiting the characteristic 'bulbous-feature' style. Other notable objects were door jambs carved in human shape and ornate spires for house roofs.

Most of Micronesia—the Mariana, Caroline, Marshall and Gilbert Islands—is coralline in formation, which encourages only a limited variety of vegetation and provides few raw materials. Micronesian societies were stratified and were composed of a mixture of Asian and Oceanic elements, linguistically diverse, but sharing common seafaring and military abilities. Most art was owned by and created for those of rank, symbolizing divisions in status between them and commoners.

Sculpture was uncommon, a few documented examples coming from the Palau and Mortlock Islands and Nukuoro. In the Palau Islands, chiefs' houses and articles of ritual importance were carved and decorated with shell inlay; reddish ochre was also used. Large white-painted masks were placed on house gables in the Mortlocks, while on Nukuoro a distinctive form of standing wood figure was created with a featureless egg-shaped head and smooth body contours. Decorative leaf textiles were plaited throughout the region.

The islands of Polynesia are the most recently settled in Oceania. Despite their wide dispersal, the inhabitants exhibited considerable cultural and linguistic homogeneity, a fact noted by Cook and others in the late 18th century. Each group possessed a stratified system of social organization in which hereditary chiefs traced their descent back to ancestral deities, thus validating their claims to authority. Polynesian religious beliefs centred on four major deities, one or more of which was recognized in each group, plus a number of lesser deities concerned with more parochial matters.

Art existed within this socio-religious framework, being created by those of high rank or by specialist 'experts', and served to demarcate social divisions—chiefs had special clothing, ornamentation and accessories. The arts also existed as a reflection of people's relationship with the supernatural, symbolized by representations of gods and ancestors and the use of sacred designs and materials. These provided physical channels through which the gods could be propitiated.

Polynesian cultural homogeneity is apparent in a number of artistic themes which occurred throughout the area. One was figure sculpture, documented examples of which have been found in all island groups except Samoa. Both male and female figures were generally repre-

This canoe prow from the Solomon Islands is inlaid with mother-of-pearl. The carved ancestor spirit offered protection in raids, and the bird was believed to keep the canoe on course.

Museum für Volkerkunde/Werner Forman Archive

sented in a standing position, with a flexed, almost squatting, stance and a disproportionately large head, and with hands placed to the sides, on the abdomen, or, on occasions, with one hand to the chin. Figures were usually kept in sacred enclosures or placed in smaller shrines.

Tattooing was another widespread art form, applied in different styles and to a varying extent on both sexes, although mainly on men. Music and dance consisted of lyrical incantations accompanied by body movements, often of the hands, arms and head performed in a sitting posture, and by the use of accessories such as drums, rattles and dance paddles. Such performances usually celebrated historical exploits and the genealogies of those of rank. The colour red had sacred significance throughout Polynesia, appearing as decoration on garments in the form of feathers, pigments or threads.

In a temperate environment, the Maoris of New Zealand developed distinctive forms in sculpture and ornamentation. Curved patterns were engraved on figure sculpture and other objects of ritual significance, such as the prow and stern sections of chiefs' canoes and footrests used with digging sticks during the annual ceremonial planting of sweet potato. Similar scrolling designs were tattooed on the faces of men of rank and the lips and chin of high ranking women. Highly

valued jade was made into ornaments, weapons and adzes, symbolic of a chief's authority. Flax-weaving techniques for making garments with decorative borders were developed in the absence of suitable materials for bark cloth manufacture.

A scarcity of suitable timber on Easter Island led to the use of stone for sculpture and the giant images created there were a development from a Polynesian stone-carving tradition, evident in the Marquesas, Society and Austral Islands. As with the small, cadaverous wood figures, the meaning of the stone sculptures is unknown, but they are probably ancestor images.

In Hawaii, wood figure sculpture was imbued with greater vigour than elsewhere in Polynesia; limbs were muscular, the head aggressive and the bulk of the body concentrated in the chest, giving a considerable impression of power. The Hawaiians also refined techniques in featherwork, creating dramatic robes for their chiefs with crescent designs worked in hundreds of thousands of yellow, red, green or black feathers. Techniques of bark cloth decoration, tattoo, music and dance were also highly developed.

In Marquesan figure sculpture, which was mainly in wood and stone, the bulk of the body was centred on the abdomen. Angular surface engraving was used and a distinctive 'spectacle-like' eye form developed. Compartmented angular designs were also the main motifs in tattoo, which in some cases covered the entire body. A wide variety of ornaments were made, mostly from ivory, feathers, shell, teeth and seeds. Large clubs with carved heads and staffs with ornamental hair pompoms were the property of noted warriors and men of rank.

The arts of the central Polynesian groups of the Society, Cook and Austral Islands were closely related. Figure sculpture here was characterized by fecund images with an emphasis on the head and abdomen. Society Islands' figures are thought to have been used in sorcery, while those from other islands usually represented deities.

The study of Oceanic art is made particularly difficult by the fact the study did not begin until contact with White people had been made, and as soon as this contact took place—and largely as a result of it—the societies under observation began to change. The introduction of metal tools sometimes led to an efflorescence of the traditional styles, as among the 19th century Maori for example, but usually the foreign influences undermined the socio-religious framework which had provided the major stimulus for indigenous art in the first place. And in the absence of written history among the natives of Oceania, the historical perspective necessary for the study of Oceanic art is hard to achieve. □

Art of the Hindu world

Hindu religion, with its rich art and complex mythology, has dominated much of Asia for the last 2,000 years, in particular the sub-continent of India and such countries as Indonesia and Cambodia. But the influence of Buddhism and Islam has also been pervasive in these areas; today only India, Nepal and Bali, and to a lesser extent Thailand and Java, are culturally Hindu.

It is impossible to understand the varied forms of Hindu art without realising that behind them lies this complex religious and social background. Hindu religion itself is paradoxical, for it contains notions of fertility, originating in the agricultural communities of rural India and tropical South-East Asia, as well as a range of philosophies which deny the reality of the everyday world and advocate the practices of transcendental discipline such as meditation and control of the body (*yoga*).

Hindu art reflects these varied preoccupations. It is composed of elements which may be described as 'folk art', belonging to the everyday cultures of the village, in combination with a truly 'high art', dominated by theology and intent upon aiding the devotee along his path towards personal liberation. Even though the visible world was dismissed by the philosophers of Hinduism as illusory (*maya*), the art of Hinduism constantly demonstrates the relevance of the visual world, both as an evocation of the forces of the cosmos, and as a reminder of the transient nature of forms.

The greatest artistic product of Hinduism was the temple, which functioned as the focal point of Hindu society both in a rural and urban setting. The temple provided a place where the gods could be approached by man, a place where the terrestrial and celestial could meet. In order to achieve a fruitful meeting, rituals of worship were evolved which are still practised today throughout India and also in Bali. Many other activities were also housed in the Hindu temple, such as those associated with the adoration of the god, which involved performing arts such as dancing, singing, instrumental music, recital of sacred texts and poetry. Drama also played an important role in temple performances, and the temple was the setting for children's education and for ceremonies of initiation, marriage and death.

In architectural style two main kinds of Hindu temple predominate. The Dravidian type, now found mainly in southern India, perhaps draws more on the very ancient principles of Indian belief before the coming of the Aryans. The spires of these temples are often arranged in a series of horizontal terraces, each of which is dedicated to a different god. Temples built in the Nagara style, mainly found in northern India, also centre on the spire, but this has a smoother curved shape.

The spires of Hindu temples were often painted white to stress the relationship with the snow-covered peaks of the Himalayas, the eternal home of the god Shiva. Temples from the 5th and 6th centuries, dedicated to the varied Hindu cults are found all over India, and also, from a slightly later period, in Java and Kampuchea. Hindu temples are still being built in both India and Bali. where the continuity of religious practice and artistic tradition has not yet been interrupted. Even the temples of South-East Asia associated with Buddhism reflect the powerful impact of building and artistic forms developed in the service of Hinduism.

There is an intimate and unique rela-

In this Trichinopoly painting women form the body of an elephant on which Kama, the god of love, is riding—a symbol of womankind seeking his favour.

Victoria & Albert Museum/Sally Chappell

2581

Amorous couples are often used as decoration in Hindu temples as here in the Kandariya Temple at Khajuraho. The couple united in a sexual act may be given deep symbolic meaning, but their protective and auspicious function is constant.

tionship between the arts of sculpture, painting and architecture in Hindu temples, for both the interiors and exteriors were richly covered with a variety of images, scenes, animals and decorative motifs. Such ornamentation was designed to provide a focus for rituals of devotion, to illustrate myths and legends and, as decoration, to be open to symbolic interpretation. This triple function reflects the different layers of Hindu social and religious life.

Images for worship are concerned with both the 'high' religion of the priests and the 'folk' religion of the village. The need for images on which to focus rituals of devotion was bound up with cults of devotional worship (*bhakti*) in which the deity is considered to be linked to his worshipper by an intimate bond. Such rituals, with their corresponding images for worship, are common throughout the Hindu world.

The art of narrative and myth reflects the popular tales of folklore. The sources of these stories—the so-called Indian Epics: the Ramayana and Mahabharata, and the collections known as the Puranas —were encyclopaedic in nature and from these came the narrative scenes that were to cover the walls of the temples of India, Thailand, Cambodia and Java. These sources also provided the material for the arts of poetry, song and dance.

The construction of most Hindu temples was undertaken as a result of royal patronage or donations by wealthy merchants. Temples were endowed in a spirit of devotion and piety and many ancient texts speak of the merit that accrues to a patron, promising him liberation. In certain circumstances, however, temples were built as a political gesture to establish the power of the ruler and the art of Hinduism thus came to be identified with the human personality of the king, the temporal representative of divine power.

As Indian culture was seldom concerned with the self-expression of the individual,

Ellen Smart

(Left) An 18th Century painting of Shiva with the sacred bull Nandi symbolising the god's agricultural aspect.

Much of Hindu Art illustrates the ancient epics, and this painting shows the monkey-god Hanuman rescuing Sita in an incident from the Ramayana.

Ellen Smart

almost all of Hindu art is anonymous. The artists whether sculptors, painters or architects were considered instruments by which things higher and greater than themselves might find expression. They thought of their work as a means of access to the divine, as is demonstrated by the amount of ancient literature describing the mental preparation and ritual purification they should undergo before commencing work. Only in this way could they identify themselves with the transcendental principles to which they would give visible form. All artists, from mastercraftsmen to journeymen, were organized into groups which functioned as guilds. These were an extension of tightly-knit family units and their artistic traditions were handed down from one generation to another.

Images and symbols of the deities are of paramount importance for Hindu devotion (*puja*). At the centre of the sanctuary of every Hindu temple, or in the sacred room of a Hindu household, beneath trees and beside rivers and lakes throughout the landscape of Hindu Asia, is placed an image or symbol which represents the deity in visible form. Subsidiary images in temples, mostly housed in wall niches, depict other aspects of the divinity. As Hindu temple architecture developed, the number of gods and goddesses placed in the walls increased; these were to inspire the worshipper as he ritually encircled the temple in a clockwise direction.

Hindu artists also illustrated myth and legend by depicting divinities in scenes

frequently taken from a climax of a story such as a god or goddess killing a demon, the rescue of a devotee from a demon's clutches or grace being bestowed upon a loyal worshipper. These scenes enabled

(*Below*) *Surrounded by maidens, Krishna bathes with the cowgirl Radha. The eighth, and most popularly worshipped incarnation of Vishnu, Krishna and his amorous adventures are celebrated in numerous paintings and poems.*

Raghubir Singh/John Hillelson Agency

Aspect

(*Above*) *The Hindu temples of Bali, of which this is the largest, are centres of teaching as well as learning. The multi-tiered wooden roofs symbolize the levels of heaven and are oriented towards the sacred mountain at the centre of Bali.*

(*Below*) *The influence of Hinduism spread from India eastward as far as Indonesia. Many legends and stories from the great epics have become the subject of shadow theatre presentation in which cut out figures represent the gods.*

William MacQuitty

Victoria & Albert Museum/John Webb

learned priests associated with the temple to explain the many Hindu myths and legends. They were also an important source of material for the performing arts. Even today in India and parts of Indonesia, Hindu myths and epic stories are acted out, danced or sung, or performed in shadow theatre—in which cut out figures represent the gods and heroes.

The imagination of the Hindu artist is best illustrated in the extraordinary range of figures that were developed to depict the divine. To this end Hindu artists drew upon human as well as animal and bird forms which they did not hesitate to mix into composite creatures. For a long time there has been a belief in India that outer forms are merely illusory and can be assumed at will be those with divine powers. Deities take a visual form simply to aid the defective imagination of their worshippers, who are unable to perform rituals of devotion without such assistance. The transient nature of the forms adopted by gods and goddesses of Hinduism is reflected in the art—the same god may be depicted in a variety of ways to suggest his many aspects. No single appearance is necessarily more significant than any other because each

may indicate the role of the deity in a particular circumstance.

The origin of the multiple forms of Hindu gods lies in the inclusive nature of Hindu cults and in their evolution. The art draws on many sources, some even non-Hindu, for the forms of these gods and goddesses, and the desire to endow male and female divine figures with obvious super-human attributes was achieved by multiplying the number of arms and heads. However when a god takes what is described as a 'human form', such as Rama and other human incarnations of Vishnu, these multiplications are abandoned.

Images of the gods had to be 'beautiful' in order to persuade the formless divine presence to inhabit them. An 'ideal' type was developed, meticulously described in the textbooks on sculpture and painting and followed by Hindu craftsmen. For male figures, shoulders and chests were to be broad, the waist slim and slightly overflowing at the belt, the limbs solid and rather cylindrical. For female figures, elaborate head-dress and jewellery, heavy breasts, a narrow waist and ample hips as well as a graceful posture were considered necessary features.

The terrible goddess Kali known as the Black One, is the destructive aspect of the Hindu Mother Goddess. This 18th century Kangra painting shows her, typically, on the battlefield.

Hindu artists never attempted to suggest the physical anatomy of figures; it was the quality of life energy or *Prana* which was important. As this was thought to be carried on the breath, the object of much religious veneration involved mastery of the breath. The figures of gods created by Hindu artists have taut-looking bodies, as if to contain a pressure from within.

One of the principal features of Hindu art is the notion of a 'vehicle' (*vahana*), usually an animal or bird, that accompanies the divine image. This vehicle is not only a means of conveyance, it also symbolizes the divine character: the bull Nandi is the agricultural aspect of Shiva and the cosmic serpent Shesha embodies Vishnu's role as creator of the universe. Animals were worshipped in India from the earliest times and the bull and snake, among others, are of the greatest significance in the folklore of Hinduism. Only later were animals and birds combined with gods and goddesses and as 'vehicles', they provided a convenient means by which divinities might be distinguished from each other. But animals and birds continued to have a life of their own in Hindu art and the depiction of elephants, lions, bulls, horses, monkeys, peacocks and ducks provide a glorious example of artistic naturalism based on direct observation of life.

The emblems held in the numerous hands of the gods and goddesses have great significance. They symbolize the power and character of the divinity and are worshipped in themselves as cult objects. The gestures of the hands (*mudras*) are considered to be particularly expressive; there is an intimate relation between Hindu sculpture and dance, in which every position of the fingers and hands signifies a detail in the telling of a story.

Facial expression is also developed by Hindu artists and in the 'ideal' female beauty the eyes are fish-like, the nose sharp and the lips thickened. Rarely, however, is there any attempt to give the gods and goddesses an outer expression; the inward-looking glance, conveying detachment from the outer world, is more characteristic. When deities are depicted in such violent pursuits as dancing or killing, Hindu artists sometimes abandon this calm expression and provide them with protruding eyes, fangs and tongues dripping with blood in an evocation of cosmic horror.

Much of Hindu art is dominated by textbooks (*shastras*) in which rules for making temples and sacred images are clearly laid out. These textbooks do not necessarily reflect the preoccupation of craftsmen; rather they are the product of theologians who set out to classify architecture and art and meticulously describe the appropriate form for each of the gods and goddesses. (This demonstrates the influence of the priestly and intellectual class upon artisans.) Proportional measurement was vital—the height and dimensional relationship of the parts of sacred buildings or the limbs of a divine image had to be carefully regulated.

In addition to the cult and folk-cult images which serve as a focus for rituals of worship, a whole host of forms and motifs add to the richness and vitality of Hindu art. Amorous couples, engaged in lovemaking or erotic acts, were carved in Hindu temples from the earliest periods. Their function is primarily auspicious and protective, and they are related to ancient secular Indian textbooks on lovemaking, such as the *Kama Sutra*. Only occasionally, however, are these figures accorded a symbolic significance in which they represent the union of man with the godhead.

Mythical creatures also play an important role. There are serpents, frequently with human torsos and reptilian bodies, as well as the mythical eagle Garuda, with a human torso, eagle wings and a beak. Throughout the Hindu art of India, Nepal, Thailand, Cambodia and Indonesia, serpents and eagles are commonly found as decorative motifs at the corners of buildings, particularly as a protective device above doorways. Celestial musicians, with bird bodies and human heads, are characteristic accessory deities, as are the dwarf-like imps (*ganas*) who guard the treasuries of precious stones. These creatures often appear in the retinues that accompany the principal god or goddess, entertaining and adoring the divinity. The imagination of Hindu artists is extensive: there is an aquatic monster depicted as a fantastic combination of crocodile and foliation, and a grotesque mask which is composed of a lion or cat-like face.

Throughout Hindu art a richness of invention is associated with a taste for the fantastic. The tendency towards the demonic is a particularly striking characteristic of the Hindu arts of the Himalayas and Indonesia, where fantastic quality is made exuberant. The aim is to provide a suitable degree of protection for sacred areas, temples or houses by keeping out unwanted visitors such as imps or evil spirits and by placating the gods and goddesses who are often worshipped in these countries in their fearful forms.

Throughout the Hindu world ornamentation based on vegetal forms is applied to sculpture, painting and even architecture. Flowers such as the lotus, depicted as a meandering stalk, a partly opened or fully opened flower, came to dominate decorative art. The lotus was particularly popular because of its significance as a symbol of perfection and enlightenment—the watery element out of which the flower grows came to func-

In all Hindu temples there is an intimate relationship between decoration and architectural form. The great temple at Shrirangam is dedicated to Vishnu: it dates from the 14th century and has an outer wall 0·8km (¹/₂ mile) long.

tion as a symbol for rebirth. The Hindu goddess of good fortune and wealth, Lakshmi, is depicted seated on a lotus whose auspicious qualities she personifies.

Other vegetal forms were transformed by Hindu artists into fantasy foliations which became pervasive throughout Hindu art. Motifs such as the vase with overflowing foliage well illustrate the fascination with foliation and the abundance associated with pots. Jewellery and garlands of flowers decorate divine figures and buildings, suggesting the qualities of abundance and wealth which Hindu craftsmen sought to bestow upon their work, and, by implication, upon their patrons. Ear pendants, multiple bracelets for arms, wrists and ankles, necklaces and elaborate belts are found everywhere.

In the art of the Hindu world form and meaning are indivisible; the bewildering range of figures with multiple limbs and heads, the hybrid creatures in which figural and animal forms are mingled and even the animal, bird and vegetal forms are all related to an elaborately structured religious system. It is an art of the sacred which celebrates the forms of nature and does not hesitate to combine them together to create powerful images. It is also an art of the everyday world which concentrates on the forces of nature, benign or demonic. By giving them visual expression it fulfils an important function for Hindu society, allowing humans to approach these aspects of the divine. Ultimately, Hindu art is aimed both at the devotees, to aid them in their path towards personal liberation, and at the invisible forces of the universe. □

Art of the Far East

For much of its long history the Far East has been comparatively isolated from the rest of the world. One of the effects of this isolation has been the evolution of a particular attitude to life and the cosmos. This has developed into a feeling that all creation is interdependent. Human beings, animals down to the smallest creature, the material world and Nature are all interconnected, reflections of each other.

These ideas are most clearly expressed in China in the teaching of Lao Tzu (605–517 BC or later) and in the composite cult which came to be called Taoism. In Japan the worship of many nature spirits was similarly brought together in a complex cult which was later called Shinto. But the same beliefs also found their way into other philosophies. The teaching of Confucius (551–475 BC) was subsequently amalgamated with many Taoist beliefs, and when Buddhism was adopted in both China and Japan, it took on many similar features.

This ccmplex of ideas underlay all Far Eastern art until comparatively modern times. Consequently, when looking at most Chinese and Japanese works of art, it is a mistake to see them in terms of one set of beliefs only. Echoes of many ideas are usually present. Rather like those late products of Chinese craft, the ivory balls-within-balls, there are onionskins of symbolism and meaning in every object.

This in turn explains another feature of Far Eastern art which might be called 'conservative adaptability'. In both China and Japan, as well as in Korea (the connecting link between the two) forms and techniques do change and new ideas are adopted. But the process often takes a considerable time and the new often carries over ideas from the old. The Chinese perhaps were more conservative in technique while being more adaptable in ideas. The Japanese were ever ready to adopt new techniques as well as ideas. But they retained old ideas and stylistic motifs for a very long time, and much is preserved in Japan that has disappeared in China and Korea. Much of the evidence for styles of early Chinese and Korean Buddhist art, for example, is now found only in Japan.

Within this context of conservatism the Japanese have tended to take new ideas further than the Chinese. There is a

CHINA		JAPAN	
Neolithic	7000-1600 BC	Early Jomon	7000-2200 BC
Shang	c.1600-1027 BC	Middle Jomon	2200-2000 BC
Chou	1027-221 BC	Late Jomon	2000-c.200 BC
Ch'in	221-206 BC		
Han	206 BC-220 AD	Yayoi	c.200 BC-c.250 AD
Six Dynasties	220-580 AD	Kofun	c.250-552 AD
Sui	580-618 AD	Asuka	522-645 AD
T'ang	618-906 AD	Nara	645-794 AD
Five Dynasties	906-960 AD	Heian	794-1185 AD
Sung	960-1279 AD	Kamakura	1185-1392 AD
Yuan	1271-1368 AD	Muromachi	1392-1568 AD
Ming	1368-1644 AD	Mamoyama	1568-1615 AD
Ch'ing (Manchu)	1644-1912 AD	Edo	1615-1868 AD
Modern Period	1912 AD on	Modern	1868 AD on
Communism	since 1949	Recent	since 1945

restraint about the Chinese character which the Japanese do not share. There is little in Chinese art to equal the violence of some of the scenes of fighting in Japanese art, or the extremely explicit eroticism of some Japanese woodblock prints. But for both peoples there remains, beneath the great variety of forms, a unity of purpose: art interprets and reflects belief. Works of art are effects, certainly, but they are also causes; art is taught but it also teaches. Especially for the Chinese scholar-artist, art was life and life was art: the world and its reflection were one.

The unity of past and present is basic to what we know of the earliest periods of Chinese history. Even in prehistoric times, when a number of late Stone Age cultures were developing around the Yellow River in North China, burial customs indicate a great reverence felt by the living for the dead. Ancestor worship remained a most important

aspect of Chinese belief up to the T'ang period. It accounts for much of the conservatism of Chinese art up to then and even up to modern times. Changes in art certainly followed changes in society, but in spite of the many violent upheavals which occurred in the course of Chinese political history, basic social patterns took a long time to change. So although the various periods of Chinese history are named after the ruling dynasties, there is a great deal of continuity between them.

The documented history of China goes back nearly 3,500 years—nearly twice as long as that of England—and archaeology is constantly extending our knowledge backwards into the past. We can divide the history of artistic development in China into three major phases based to some extent on differences in the general artistic media employed. The first phase correlates with the Bronze Age, and its most significant products are the ceremonial bronzes of the Shang and Chou Dynasties. The roots of this Bronze Age are to be found in the late neolithic cultures that flourished in the Yellow River valley. As Chinese society evolved from the wandering nomadic tribes to the first large urban settlements, art shifted from pottery making to bronze casting.

About 2500 BC the first bronzes of high artistic quality were cast, probably after centuries of experimentation. Until almost the first century AD these bronzes were the major artistic expression of the Chinese. In the many vessels, weapons, chariot fittings and items of personal adornment from these early centuries, we can perhaps trace the development of a society as it moved from an overwhelming concern with superstition and magic to an involvement with personal power and glory.

The earliest bronzes, those of the Shang Dynasty, were almost all used in rituals involving ancestor worship. The precise laws governing Shang rituals are still unknown, but from the decoration of the bronze vessels we may guess that the ceremonies were complex and of a serious and sacred nature. The vessels were made

(Right) In this marble stele of the Six Dynasties period, Sakyamuni, the Buddha, is shown between disciples and Bodhisattvas. Buddhism had profound effects on Chinese art for hundreds of years.

(Below) This Chou bronze wine vessel is inscribed: 'For the august Father Six Days, a precious ritual vessel to be placed in the ancestral temple, to be treasured in prominent use for a myriad years and in perpetuity by sons and grandsons'.

Robert Harding/Robert Harding Associates/T.N.L.

Derrick Witty/Robert Harding Associates/T.N.L.

in many forms, the most common being for pouring and drinking wine. They were elaborately decorated, with images of dragons, beasts, birds and serpents placed in relief against a background consisting of repeated spirals.

The symbol of a type of animal mask called the *t'ao-t'ieh* was of special importance and appears in varying stylized forms on most of the ritual bronzes of the Shang period. Sometimes called a monster mask, or a glutton mask, the *t'ao-t'ieh* seems to sum up the basic qualities of early Chinese art: mysterious, visually complicated, elaborate and compelling.

In the later stages of bronze art, when the Chou Empire was breaking up in the period known as the Warring States (roughly the 5th to 2nd centuries BC), inscriptions on the vessels tell us of many different uses for the bronzes. Vessels were cast as rewards for meritorious

deeds, battles fought and won, recognition of rank, or to celebrate special occasions such as weddings.

The visual qualities of the bronzes also changed, as Chinese society moved away from constant ritual worship toward the celebration of secular power and began to seek prestige. The fierce *t'ao-t'ieh*, the complex imagery of beasts and the mysterious spiral background motifs are replaced by the heavy use of inlay, using stones such as turquoise or precious metals such as gold or silver. A rich interlacing of geometric scrolls appears on the surface to help dazzle the eye and to overwhelm the senses. When animal forms appear in the later bronzes, they have a realistic cast to them and often involve such scenes as the hunt or specific animals like the lion.

The Shang period was one in which ritual was complex and the rules determining the design of bronze vessels

Claus Hansmann

domesticated animals like pigs and chickens all take their place alongside those of servants and court officials. Made rapidly from clay and often left unpainted, the tomb figurines of these centuries capture with their lively spirit the exuberance of a society that had moved a long way from its pre-occupation with matters of ritual and ancestor worship.

The second major phase of Chinese art corresponds with the age of Buddhism. The religion that was ultimately to spread over all East Asia had come to China during the Han period, but it was not until the 4th century AD that images of the great deity appeared in any quantity. By the 5th century, however, Buddhism had spread over most of the northern regions of China and accounted for much

(Left) A camel with a Central Asian rider in three-coloured glaze from an early 8th century T'ang tomb. Such figures helped the dead to continue a life in the spirit world similar to that on earth.

(Below) The Mongol conquest of China in the late 13th century set up the Yuan dynasty, and introduced a new vigour in art. This eight-sided pot is decorated under the glaze with blue dragons.

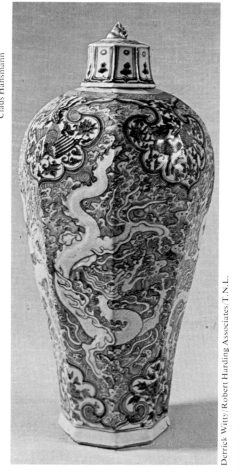

Derrick Witty/Robert Harding Associates/T.N.L.

appear to have been both complex and rigid. During the Chou period, this rigidity appears to have relaxed into a greater freedom in design. It is probable that this reflects an opening outward of the world of the artist, perhaps running parallel with changes in social organization. When the Chou empire began to break up at the end of the 8th century BC, there was considerable social and political confusion. The teachings of both Lao Tzu and Confucius were attempts to restore order to a world which suddenly seemed chaotic, and from this time on Taoism and Confucianism had an important effect on Chinese art.

The very last stage of bronze culture merged with what might be called the iron age in China during the Han Dynasty. With iron came agricultural implements and a different way of asserting control over the environment. Superstition and magic, although always present to some degree, were less important in the art that reflects Han society. Painting in

lacquer, sculpture in stone and wood, and pottery figurines and vessels began to appear in substantial numbers as indicators of a growing wealth that was widely dispersed geographically.

Excavations in recent years of Han tombs found all over China have brought to light the extensive use of *ming-ch'i*, or objects placed in the grave as substitution for real things in the spirit world. Most of the *ming-ch'i* were put in tombs of noblemen whose families furnished the grave with all the necessary paraphernalia to assure the tranquility of the soul in the afterworld. Included among the objects were figures of warriors and exorcists to take care of evil-doers, and dancers and musicians to provide for entertainment.

Although it was only the well-to-do who could command such attention from their families, what is interesting to observe in the *ming-ch'i* of the Han is the wide-spread interest in agriculture. Models of farmyards, storehouses and

Claus Hansmann

of the artistic production of the Chinese craftsman. Until the extensive persecutions of Buddhism in the 9th century, the religion dominated the hearts and minds of millions of Chinese, supplying them with a strong focus for their artistic energy as well as for their spiritual and intellectual needs.

The multitudes of images of the Buddha and other deities in the pantheon must have seemed overwhelming to the Chinese, who had little experience of the idea of worshipping icons. Neither Confucianism, with its strict codes of ethical social behaviour and conduct as related through the words of a teacher, nor Taoism, with its mystical overtones and stress on such vague concepts as intuitive awareness, could be readily translated by the artist into concrete symbols. Buddhism, however, provided the Chinese artist with a well-developed panoply of images, cast into a recognizable form.

From the temples at Yun-kang to those of Lung-men (near Loyang) of the 6th and 7th centuries, we can trace in stone the visual record of Buddha's conquest of China. Thousands of images were chiselled out of rock through these centuries; many thousands more were cast in bronze, modelled in clay, carved in wood, or painted on silk or paper. Buddhist art was, in the best sense of the word, mass-produced for the largest possible audience; it came as close as art ever has in China

(Above) A carved wooden 'flying horse' of the Sung period demonstrates the conservatism which runs through Chinese art. Similar subjects are shown later in Han bronzes and in 18th century jewellery.

(Below) This 18th century appliqué-work fan is decorated with a dragon and a pearl, representing the Taoist principles of Ying and Yang —symbols for female and male which recur in Chinese art.

Claus Hansmann

Werner Forman Archive/Pullan Collection

The scholar-artist had a profound effect on Chinese painting. This Ming period painting shows a landscape—always a popular choice for expressing the refined poetic sensibilities of a class to whom both Taoist and Ch'an Buddhist ideas were of great importance.

Bearded dignitaries from Persia, horsemen from Mongolia and tradesmen from Korea and Japan all became the subject of endless fascination for the tomb artist.

The decline of Buddhism as the great vital force in the arts probably began somewhere around the mid-8th century as the courtly arts began to claim more and more attention from artists. Although the persecutions of the 9th century destroyed a great deal of Buddhist art, particularly the temples in the major cities, and effectively ended the main period of artistic flourishing for the religion, Buddhism continued to exert some influence on Chinese art.

The last vigorous movement of Chinese Buddhist art came with the spread of Ch'an or Zen Buddhism (as it is called in Japan). Beginning during the T'ang dynasty, Ch'an spread widely in China towards the end of the Sung dynasty at the end of the 12th and the beginning of the 13th centuries. The words Ch'an and Zen both derive from the Sanskrit word *dhyana*, meaning meditation. Ch'an began as a rediscovery of 'basic' Buddhism in reaction to the over-ceremonial and logic-chopping manner in which institutional Buddhism had developed. It aimed at attaining a state of inner enlightenment, the Buddha-nature inherent in each individual. Once this state had been achieved every action would become a manifestation of ultimate truth.

Hundreds of gilded images were of little help in attaining this goal: painting that emphasized simplicity and spontaneity was a far more suitable vehicle. Ch'an turned the intellectuals who practised both calligraphy and representational painting away from the previous elaboration and richness of style towards a more direct technique and a vision of the world which has a sparse, stripped-down look, concentrating on essentials. It was a style which could easily be combined with Taoist objectives, and it became a popular means of expression among the scholar-artists.

Overlapping in time with this last flourishing of Buddhist art in China is the third important phase of Chinese art,

Due to their fragile nature, no screens of great antiquity have survived, but this 18th century Chinese screen exemplifies the continuous Chinese interest in nature's minutiae.

(until very recent times) to being a true people's art. The actual images varied considerably, from the linear, floating forms of the early 6th century to the fully three-dimensional full-bodied forms of the 8th century, but there is no doubting the great fervour and spiritual energy.

The influence of Buddhist sculptural forms had great implications for non-Buddhist art as well. Nowhere was this experience better utilized than in the production of tomb figurines during the

T'ang Dynasty. Just as Buddhist art of this age is the art of the people, the tomb figures of the T'ang capture something of the flavour of court life.

In addition to illustrating the lavish splendour of court life in the 7th and 8th centuries, the tomb figures also record with accuracy the diversity and complexity of the large metropolitan centres of Chinese civilization: in their streets camel drivers from Central Asia mingled with wine merchants from Armenia.

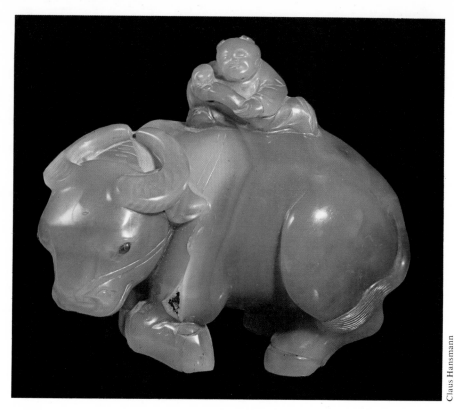

Claus Hansmann

which may be equated with the emergence of painting as the major means of artistic expression. Although painting had played a significant role in Chinese art as early as the Han dynasty, and was important also to T'ang artists, it was not until the Sung period that painting became dominant. This dominance continued through the periods of the Ming dynasty and the Manchus to modern times.

Justified in Sung theoretical writing as the appropriate activity for the man of superior intellect, painting became, like poetry, one of the accomplishments of the scholar. It was no longer the exclusive province of the professional artist and it was combined with calligraphy as well as poetry as a means by which the intellectual élite conveyed their special feelings. Taoism and Confucianism played an important part in this new aesthetic theory, and landscape became a favoured subject because it provided a 'pure' vehicle for the expression of poetic sensibility. The hold that the scholar-artists maintained on the world of Chinese art from Sung times until the 17th century is evident in the many examples of delicate, often monochromatic landscape paintings. It was an art for an élite, and was never intended to have a popular or general appeal.

In the later centuries, Chinese art once again featured the craftsman. The sumptuous carved jades of the 17th and 18th centuries, the marvellous ceramics produced from the Sung dynasty onwards, the intricate lacquer-work, the enamels and gold and silver objects of extraordinary workmanship, all show the affluence

(Above) Jade was valued by the Chinese for its medicinal and preservative qualities. The man on the back of this 19th century carved buffalo carries a ju-i sceptre, a Taoist sexual symbol.

(Below) Haniwa figures like this were placed in the great tumulus tombs of the Japanese emperors of the Yayoi period. They probably had a similar purpose to Chinese funerary figures in serving the dead.

Werner Forman Archive/Seattle Art Museum

of the royal and official classes who ordered them. Emperors and high court officials became passionate collectors of all kinds of objects, with which they decorated their palaces and studios. These learned and cultivated men continued to paint and write poetry themselves: collecting and connoisseurship contributed to these pursuits and became an end in themselves. By the 17th century complex theories about art had emerged, along with an art-for-art's-sake approach to painting. In technical terms some 18th and 19th century products of the Ch'ing period are unsurpassed.

The peninsula of Korea lies between China and Japan, and has at different times been subject to each of them. The Koreans regularly absorbed Chinese ideas and techniques and then proceeded to alter and to refine them. The peninsula served as a funnel down which these altered ideas passed to Japan; indeed until the establishment of direct diplomatic relations between Japan and China in the T'ang period, Korea regularly performed this function. Of particular importance was the occasion in the year 552 AD when the Paekche king of Kudara in South Korea sent an ambassador to ask for military assistance from Japan.

The ambassador brought to the Japanese court as presents a small image of the Buddha and some scriptures. The progressives favoured accepting the new faith, while the more conservative resisted it, and a conflict developed which took several years to settle. It was eventually resolved in favour of Buddhism, but only after considerable fighting, and the traditionalist beliefs in Shinto were never eliminated.

Much Korean art of the Old Silla kingdom and the Paekche period is particularly distinguished in its elegant simplified line and its air of quiet tranquility. Both these qualities influenced the earliest Japanese Buddhist art of the late 6th and early 7th centuries. Similarly, the beauty and technical skill of the pottery of the Koryo period also influenced Japan. These are only two examples of the countless ways in which Korean influence carried mainland ideas across the water to Japan, and it is probable that further instances will be found as more evidence is uncovered by archaeology.

At present, it must be admitted, information about the origins and purposes of the earliest Japanese art is scanty. For over 7,000 years up to the 2nd century BC there flourished all over Japan a culture called Jomon. The name derives from the cord pattern found on the many earthenware vessels and ritual figurines which the culture produced. There is a violence about these objects, an air of fantasy in the shapes and patterns employed, which is quite extraordinary.

Coils of clay are added to the surface and combined with incised and impressed decoration to make a lively sculptured effect. The exact function which some of the objects performed for the hunters and fishermen who made them is not known. The figures of humans and animals, *dogu*, seem to have had a ritual importance, but exactly what this was remains obscure.

Towards the end of the second century BC, rice cultivation was brought to Japan from the mainland and this led to the formation of the Yayoi culture which lasted until the middle of the 3rd century AD. Metal working, both bronze and iron, was also introduced and was used, for example, to make ritual bells called *dotaku*. Yayoi pottery is quieter, plainer and more restrained than that of the Jomon period. It has a formal beauty and a degree of control in which surface decoration is subordinated to form and function. The rationality of Yayoi makes a strong contrast with the slightly mad feeling of some Jomon work, even though there is some technical continuity between the two. It is tempting to describe Yayoi as the peaceful, feminine, counterpart of the more warlike, masculine Jomon— a feature observed in other parts of the world as hunting societies give way to agriculture.

As also happened elsewhere, the development of agriculture led to the formation of centralized political auth-

(Above) The end of the Heian period from which this painting dates was marked by chaos. Feudal warlords seized power, and militarism remained part of Japanese thought and art.

(Below) The palaces built by the warlords of the Momoyama period contained sumptuous screens painted in gold leaf. The technique continued in the Edo period but the subject matter changed.

Victoria & Albert Museum/Michael Holford

Claus Hansmann

ority. From the end of the Yayoi period Japan was unified under more powerful emperors, whose large tumulus mound tombs, *kofun*, give their name to the next period. The Tomb period lasted from about 250 AD to the middle of the 6th century when Buddhism was introduced. The mounds themselves began as circular piles over the tomb but they later acquired extensive platforms in front which gave them a characteristic keyhole shape. The largest were surrounded with moats such as can still be seen around the tumulus of the Emperor Nintoku at Osaka.

Many objects were buried in the tombs, including human figures, *haniwa*, with a similar function to that of Chinese tomb figures. They are made of an unglazed earthenware in a clear and direct, rather stylized cylindrical manner. Other pottery, Sue ware, is grey and fired to a high temperature. It represents a fusion of native Japanese earthenware techniques with more advanced methods imported from Silla Korea. Metalwork too is much influenced by the mainland—Chinese dragons, for example, are a common motif. Arms and armour, horse-trappings, mirrors and personal ornaments all attest to the growing power and wealth of the rulers.

Buddhism brought with it to Japan many of the arts and techniques which it had picked up in the course of its 1,000-year journey from India. Up to this point many of the Japanese nature-beliefs which were later called Shinto (the Way of the Gods) to distinguish them from the 'Way of Buddha', had found only occasional expression in art. Wooden spirit-shrines were built, but the spirits, *kami*, themselves were not usually represented. The elaborate iconography which came with Buddhism may therefore have been an added attraction of the new faith which came to dominate Japanese art with considerable intensity until the 11th century. Japan did not experience the persecutions of Buddhism which ravaged China in the 9th century and so the influence of this religion on Japanese art continued even after this high point, right up to the present day.

The first Buddhist period in Japan, the Asuka, lasted from 552 to 645 and the spread of the religion was largely due to the Regent-Prince Shotoku. The heads of many of the ruling families adopted Buddhism and vied with one another in building magnificent temples, whose main function was to house the many images of the Buddha. The earliest temples still preserve examples of Korean and Chinese styles which have disappeared on the mainland.

During the Nara period, at the end of the 7th century, the Japanese opened up direct diplomatic relations with T'ang China. Japanese art had been com-

(Above) The subjects depicted in Edo art suited the prosperous middle class of a busy town. Courtesans feature frequently in woodblock prints like this one by Kunisada.

(Below) This netsuke shows the Dragon King of the Sea with the Tide-Jewel in his hand. His daughter married the Fire Fade Prince and their grandson was the first Emperor of Japan.

paratively simple before the introduction of Buddhism. The glories of T'ang China must have been overwhelming and many aspects of Chinese art such as the honeysuckle motif were adopted. In characteristic fashion they were given a convincingly Japanese feel. Certainly the Japanese have always 'borrowed' in art, but the process is one of absorption and digestion, not merely of imitation.

A particularly glorious monument to the art of the Nara period is still to be seen in the Shosoin. This is a storehouse, built in the grounds of the Todaiji temple to house the 600 objects dedicated to the Buddha by the widow of the emperor who built the temple. The contemporary catalogue and subsequent additions give us a remarkable record of this great period of Japanese Buddhist art.

Once official embassies to China had ceased, direct Chinese influence on Japanese art declined. In the following period, the Heian, an unmistakably indigenous style began to take shape. The capital was moved to Heian-Kyo, (Kyoto), and a growing taste for refinement emerged among the aristocracy of the court. Objects such as inlaid lacquer boxes and decorated papers for writing poetry began to occupy artistic attention and developed in a restrained and formal manner typical of the best Japanese design. The Taira scrolls and the boxes containing them, which date from the latter part of the Heian period, are breath-taking in their elegance.

The aristocracy adopted a particularly Japanese sect of Buddhism, the Jodo or 'Pure Land' sect. It was dominant among them by the time the Fujiwara family took control of the empire in about 1000 AD. In obedience to its gently forgiving doctrines they built earthly replicas of the Paradise of Amida Buddha: the Phoenix Hall in the Byodoin temple at Uji, south of Kyoto, is a magnificent example. It is unsurpassed in opulence—a riot of decoration from floor to ceiling—employing a wide variety of techniques. Rather like the officials in Sung China, the Heian aristocrats devoted great attention to the cultivation of their romantic sensibilities, delighting in motifs drawn from nature like birds in marshes, flowers and the passing of the seasons. Calligraphy was valued also, a magnificent example being the Anthology of the Thirty-Six Poetic Geniuses, produced in the early 12th century by the finest calligraphers in Kyoto.

Towards the end of the 12th century Heian control collapsed in a succession of bloody civil wars which were brought to an end by the establishment of the Shogunate. The emperors remained in Kyoto as the divine source of ritual and ceremonial power, but political power passed to the Shoguns at Kamakura. The Shoguns saw the extravagant luxury

René Burri/Magnum

Zen Buddhism became the most common belief among the Samurai warrior class of Japan. The religion had a profound effect on the design of Japanese gardens: ordered simplicity was seen as an aid to meditation.

of the Heian period as largely responsible for this chaos. They renewed contact with China and introduced a more austere controlled morality.

The Samurai code of honour was designed to foster a spirit of absolute self-control among their feudal followers. They adopted the teachings of Ch'an Buddhism, which as Zen in Japan became something quite different from its original Chinese form. Natural 'rightness' and spontaneity were applied to a military code of behaviour, in blatant disregard of the basic Buddhist prohibition of all killing. Many senior Zen monks were also members of the Samurai caste.

The favoured technique of painting became, as a result, a restrained ink monochrome. Ch'an masterpieces from China were eagerly collected. In many aspects of Japanese art, the softness, sentimentality and nostalgia of the Heian period were replaced in the Kamakura by a new decisiveness and a forceful realism. A feeling of order, severity and intellectualism is strongly perceptible in such objects as the brilliant lacquer boxes produced at this time. Zen also

brought with it the tea ceremony, which had a great influence on Japanese life and art, particularly in ceramics, and this influence continued to grow during the succeeding Muromachi period. Gardens also became an important focus for Zen art.

At the end of the 16th century there occurred a short but critical period, the Momoyama. Established society once again collapsed in chaos and political disunity, and a new order was created out of the ruins in an economic, political and social transformation of amazing speed. Warlords of great but fleeting power built magnificent palaces and filled them with marvellous objects. Large wall spaces and huge screens were covered in sumptuous decoration, often painted on gold leaf. The design of kimonos and costumes for the Noh theatre gained a similar magnificence. European influence began to be felt and Portuguese merchants, for example, began to be portrayed. Ceramics continued to develop, especially for the tea ceremony.

From the beginning of the 17th to the middle of the 19th centuries the capital of Japan was at Edo, the modern Tokyo. Trade brought great wealth to a new class, the merchants and the urban middle classes, who had little sympathy with previous aristocratic, military or Zen ideals. They demanded an art which reflected their own lives, the life of a busy

metropolitan city with its theatres, prostitutes and markets.

Thus while an efficient feudal system maintained order, and orthodoxy continued to flourish at Kyoto, Edo became a lively, fashion-conscious bourgeois alternative. To satisfy popular taste painting adopted a wholly different subject-matter, and eventually a new technique, that of wood-block printing by which pictures could be produced for a mass market. It is these prints which are best known of all Japanese art in the West. Other arts also flourished, with the traditional Japanese care in design and skill in manufacture. Decorative metalwork was used for the *ojime* buttons which secured the *inro* boxes carried on a cord at the waist. The boxes themselves and the buttons, *netsuke*, which secured the waist end of the cord were frequently miniature masterpieces in lacquer and ivory.

In 1868 the feudal political structure of the Shogunate was replaced by the restored power of the Emperor. Meiji (Emperor from 1867 to 1912) introduced the 'Western Cultural Enlightenment'— a phase of cultural importation which still continues. Japanese society has become mainly industrial, but the same processes go on. Techniques are taken up from everywhere, but the result is a peculiarly Japanese amalgam in which the traditions of the past still play an important part. ☐

The Hammer and the Sickle

Lenin's Bolshevik party seized power in Russia in October 1917, following the abdication of the Czar earlier that year. By 1921, at the end of the Civil War, they had largely consolidated their power over the old Czarist empire and a series of constitutional initiatives followed, aimed at setting up a federal structure which while formally recognizing ethnic and territorial distinctions within that empire would be in practice severely limited by the strictures of socialist ideology on nationalism and nationalities.

The 15 major republics that form the present-day Soviet Union have a total population of 268,825,000. Each republic is divided into numerous components of varying administrative status which partly take account of the range of ethnic groupings which lie within their borders.

Immediately after 1917 and during the Civil War of 1918–21 the Bolsheviks sought support in every area of the old Czarist empire and this led them to abandon the time-honoured Russian chauvinism of the pre-revolutionary era. Instead, national and ethnic minorities were encouraged to follow socialist policies in political, cultural and economic affairs, as long as this was consistent with Lenin's policy of 'democratic centralism'. The party, and Lenin himself, tried to reduce Russian domination of other nationalities in pursuance of a unified supranational state. Special resolutions to that effect were passed at the 10th and 12th Party Congresses in 1921 and 1923. Local languages were supported for use in general literacy and educational programmes. The Arabic script used by Turkic languages like Azerbaidzhani, Kazakh, Tajik or Tatar was replaced by Latin and some 50 or more small minority groups received a specially devised written language. Russian was not to be enforced as the first language in education.

After Lenin's death in 1924 Stalin promoted Russian nationalism to the full and deliberately encouraged the Russians to exert a dominant influence over all other national groups within the Soviet Union. Russian bureaucrats gradually flooded the republics, Russian increasingly became the primary language of education and administration, and Cyrillic script replaced Latin in all but the Georgian and Armenian republics. In the purges of the late 1930s leading nationalists and

party personnel from all the union republics were imprisoned and executed, while vigorous anti-religious policies were pursued in an attempt to secularize the traditional Moslem communities of Central Asia—a policy initiated under Lenin.

Stalin's reasons for acting in this manner may initially have been economic, but he also appears to have feared the rise of nationalist sentiment and discontent amongst the non-Russian population. During the Second World War this led him to deport whole groups, such as the Crimean Tatars, the Chechens, the Volga Germans and others to remote areas of the Soviet Union. Only after Stalin's death was any attempt made to modify the harshest of his policies, but even so, the generally accepted line of Russification was far from dropped in 1953 and has proceeded in less obvious and drastic ways ever since. Neither the Crimean Tatars nor the Volga Germans were included in the national groups repatriated in 1957, nor subsequently.

Since 1917 three major developments have taken place in the Soviet Union, two of which are direct results of socialist policy, the third reflecting world economic and technological trends. These are, first, a crash programme of industrialization begun in 1928; second, the collectivization of agriculture dating from the same year. The third is a more general tendency which embraces several different areas: improved travel facilities (better roads and railways, air travel), improved medicare, educational and communications media (radio, TV via satellite or internal network) and an increasing emphasis on economic self-reliance, especially in raw materials of strategic importance. All of these processes have led to greater population mobility, cultural interpenetration and a need to realise the economic potential of vast areas of the Soviet Union.

Present trends, based on the most recent census (1979) indicate that there has been large scale migration of Russians to the peripheral areas of the Soviet Union. Russian predominance is being steadily extended as a result of carefully planned educational and publishing expansion, the migration of industrial and agricultural settlers, and an employment policy under which special bonuses are paid to workers who leave European

Richard Harrington/Camera Press

Henri Cartier-Bresson/John Hillelson Agency

(*Above left*) *The Soviet Union's massive industrialization programme has meant greater material prosperity for many and changed the position of women, particularly in Moslem communities.*

(*Left*) *Exploitation of the Soviet Union's vast natural resources is usually controlled by Russian technicians, and always financed from Moscow. These pipelines constructed in Yakutsk stretch symbolically westwards.*

(*Above right*) *Oil derricks near Baku on the Caspian Sea are part of an industry of crucial importance to the Soviet Union. The Soviet emphasis on industrial expansion makes the exploitation of natural resources a high priority.*

(*Below*) *Despite many advances, Soviet agriculture is less efficient than required. Initial resistance to collectivization in some areas was ruthlessly suppressed, and millions of kulaks were transported.*

Novosti

Emil Schulthess/Transworld Feature Syndicate

Russia to take up jobs in distant areas. Large cities have grown up in republican capitals like Tashkent, Alma-Ata and Tbilisi, or in areas of advanced industrial development like northern Kazakhstan, Siberia and the Far East where urban growth has been considerable. Large numbers of Russians have moved there with official backing from Moscow, but it is not only Russians who are attracted to them by the prospect of better jobs and housing.

During the Soviet period as a whole there has been a marked population drift from countryside to city with often disastrous consequences for agriculture. This has brought about profound changes in rural life. And latterly, the influx of Russian industrial workers has brought the non-Russian population into con-

tention with Russians, in both Central Asia and Siberia.

In the meantime, it seems, there is a growing tendency for smaller ethnic groups like the Bashkirs, Karakalpaks and Abkhazians to be gradually absorbed into the larger Tatar, Kazakh and Georgian units around them. In consequence, national minorities have become more streamlined and the USSR's slender majority of Russians are being confronted at Union level by fewer, but more powerful ethnic groups. This process represents a latent challenge to the traditional dominant status of the Russians which in turn has led to a strong revival of Russian nationalism in recent years.

While Moscow remains the centre of administrative power and much of the technological impetus of the USSR comes from Russians, there has been a noticeable resurgence of national identity in other union republics such as the Baltic states, Georgia, the Ukraine and the Central Asian Republics. Traditional Russian dominance, associated so much with Stalin's regime, may be undermined by the falling Russian birthrate compared to much higher levels in the Moslem republics of Central Asia—a demographic disparity with considerable political significance.

Nationalism within the union republics takes two distinct forms. In places like the Baltic republics, Armenia, Georgia or the Ukraine it is based on a longstanding sense of cultural and historical unity— usually predating the foundation of the old Russian state itself. Such revived national feeling centres on resentment at Russian dominance and cultural penetration at all levels. Other areas owe their sense of unity not just to this kind of resentment, but paradoxically, to the very changes in their way of life that have been brought about by the formation of the Soviet Union: urbanization, industrialization, education and literacy, and changes in the rural economy. In such areas national consciousness has tended to develop around republican capitals, regional centres of administration, universities and the communications media.

In the Baltic republics—Lithuania, Estonia and Latvia—annexed in 1940, national feeling has focussed on anti-Russian sentiment caused by the manner of their incorporation into the USSR. Purges, deportations of so-called kulaks (or prosperous farmers and peasants), intellectuals and religious leaders (expecially in Catholic Lithuania), has caused immeasurable harm to the economies and social life of these areas, and has stiffened their resistance to Russification. All three republics are being progressively industrialized (especially Latvia) and enjoy a good standard of living compared to the rest of the Soviet Union. Estonia preserves its language, folklore, religion and its traditional song festivals, which have become occasions for outbursts of national feeling. Lithuania has remained staunchly Catholic and demands for greater religious freedom and tolerance led to serious riots in the town of Kaunas during the 1970s.

Georgia and Armenia both have a long cultural history and have developed a strongly independent social structure and religious tradition. Contact with Russia has not meant that Armenians have entirely abandoned their traditional life and customs. Their Apostolic Church remains extremely influential, permitted to flourish, perhaps, in order to maintain links with the large number of Armenians abroad, especially in the US. Many Georgians retain their Orthodox faith and their love of huge feasts to celebrate weddings,

Novosti

C. M. Dixon

(*Above*) *A poster in Bokhara, Uzbekistan, shows Lenin conferring with Asiatic minority leaders. But his policy of democratic centralism degenerated into Russian dominance under Stalin—a Georgian.*

birthdays or funerals. Both affect a certain scorn for the Russians whom they regard as culturally inferior.

The Ukraine, which has become increasingly industrialized during the Soviet period, suffered most noticeably from the effects of collectivization—the famine of 1933 being the culmination of the process. During the 1930s its party and intellectuals were ruthlessly purged and popular armed resistance to the Russians continued into the early 1950s. In recent years there has been a spirited revival of national feeling, centred on demands for greater political and cultural autonomy, and resentment against cul-

tural Russification and anti-national policies. These have generally been dealt with severely by the authorities, drastic prison sentences being inflicted on Ukranian dissidents for example.

Religion has generally played an important role in focussing national discontent in the Soviet Union since Stalin's death. This is notably true of the Moslem areas in Central Asia where resistance to Russification may not be so open, but traditional values and attitudes are still very strong. Even in the Russian republic itself the rise of national feeling since the death of Stalin has been marked by renewed interest in Christianity. It is

Novosti

Novosti

(*Above*) *Since the Revolution literacy has spread throughout Russia. These reindeer herders are looking at periodicals in the bookshop of the Levozersky collective.*

(*Above left*) *Although Russians still predominate in most professional occupations, members of minorities also receive training. Vasily Konstantinov is a Yakut who graduated from flying school.*

(*Below*) *Moslem Tajik pray in the mosque at Dushanbe. Most are orthodox Sunnis of the Hanafi school. In spite of Communist opposition to religion, Islam still flourishes in Central Asia.*

(*Above*) *At the boarding-school of Ekonda trading station in Siberia, children of Evenki hunters and reindeer herders are taught by a Russian teacher. Education has advanced Russification.*

(*Below*) *Jews meeting in a Leningrad synagogue on a Saturday. Jews have suffered from varying degrees of oppression in Soviet Russia: many have emigrated but exit visas are often hard to obtain.*

Novosti

Henri Cartier-Bresson/John Hillelson Agency

significant that the so-called dissident movement' of recent years has drawn much of its strength from areas like the Ukraine and the Baltic republics where national feeling is strong and explicit. Groups such as the Crimean Tatars are pressing for belated justice through this movement and Georgian Jews are among the most numerous emigrants to Israel in the last few years.

Traditional 'Russian' expansion during the Soviet period has proceeded side-by-side with the industrial development of the USSR following the First Five-Year Plan of 1928–32. During this 'construction' phase, and again after the Second

World War, there was strong emphasis on industrial development throughout the Soviet Union. Coal, oil, iron ore, tin, uranium, precious metals and timber have been exploited in various regions, promoted by Russian expertise, always funded from Moscow.

New towns and cities were founded in the Far East, Siberia, the Caucasus and Central Asia. The communications serving them, in particular the newly established air network, have brought previously primitive and far-flung communities into direct contact with Russian and European technological and scientific ideas.

The most obvious consequences of the

sweeping Soviet education programme begun under *Narkompros* immediately after the revolution have been the spread of literacy throughout the territory of the Union, accompanied by intense Russian cultural assimilation (notably in the Ukraine), greater mobility in employment and the chance of greater material prosperity for a large cross-section of the population. The position of women, particularly in Moslem communities like the Uzbeks, has been basically changed by the removal of traditional taboos against the employment of women outside the home. Yet the very processes which have led to the breakdown of local

Novosti

In recent years there has been a resurgence of national identity in many union republics. This public building in Alma-Ata, named after Lenin, was designed by Kazakhs.

traditional social structures and values have also made a sense of national or linguistic identity doubly important and have fostered a deeper cultural unity in the non-Russian republics. In places like Uzbekistan and Kazakhstan this has led to a revival of interest in local rituals, festivals and traditional dress.

Soviet technological progress, initiated by the emphasis on heavy industrialization during Stalin's time, has been considerable but inadequate in certain sectors to meet the demands of the day, as with the Western Siberia petroleum industry. The

Siberia has been deeply affected by major socialist programmes of industrialization and collectivization. Improvements in transport have brought all parts of the Union under greater central control.

agricultural policy, based in the collectivism carried out between 1928 and the mid-thirties, has been less of a success. Initial resistance to collectivization, especially in the Kazakh and Kirghiz areas of traditional nomad herdsmen, was ruthlessly suppressed under Stalin. The campaign against the kulaks led to millions of people being uprooted and transported to inhospitable regions of the Soviet Union. Even now, Soviet agriculture, for all its advances, still does not function as efficiently as required, and in some years grain has to be imported.

Central policies first developed by Kruschev and his successors have aimed at opening up hitherto undeveloped tracts of the Soviet hinterland. Where this has occurred mechanized agricultural methods have had profound effects on the environment and pattern of life of com-

munities, particularly in the 'virgin lands' of Kazakhstan, now the second breadbasket of the Soviet Union.

The present-day Soviet Union has become with the years a multi-national Russian-administered empire that aims at becoming, through merging the nationalities, an homogeneous state. Culture contact within its boundaries must be seen in terms of this complicated objective. Though they are only 53.7 per cent of the Soviet Union's total population, Russians make up over 60 per cent of both party leadership and party membership. They exercise considerable power in republican administrations through membership of republican party organizations, deputy secretaryships and chairmanships of republican KGB (secret police) apparatus and the regional defence organizations. Specialists and skilled personnel in the Soviet Union still tend to be predominantly Russian. Russian is still thought of as the first language of the USSR and increasingly as the 'native language' of non-Russian peoples.

Russian cultural assimilation continues apace through the Russian dominated media. It remains to be seen how much influence the separate republics will in future be able to exert in spite of these assimilation-merging aims of Soviet policy.

Howard Sochurek/John Hillelson Agency

The Fatal Impact

It is only in the last two hundred years that the Western world has known of the many islands which lie scattered over the vast area of the Pacific Ocean. Although individual islands were discovered by the early sailors who circumnavigated the globe in the 17th century, detailed knowledge dates from the three major voyages of the English navigator Captain Cook.

Cook was the first white man to visit the island of Hawaii, and his reception there was extraordinary. His visit was taken for the promised return of the god Lono, and the people fell on their faces on the shore in front of him. Even at his death in 1779, the year after his first visit to the Hawaiian islands, he was still treated as a divine being: his body was divided up with the greatest respect, burnt and the bones carefully scraped and preserved.

Not all Pacific Islanders welcomed the newcomers so enthusiastically. But many were friendly, and suffered greatly for their friendliness. Contemporary European thought, particularly the political philosophy of the time, made much of the idea of the 'Noble Savage'. Only 20 years before, Jean Jacques Rousseau had described an ideal situation with humans in their original state, uncorrupted by civilization.

Cook's reactions to the ordered life, the comparative freedom from hard work which life on a fertile tropical island made possible, and his ignorance of the harder aspects of life on some of the islands encouraged him to describe Tahiti, for example, as 'a golden isle of blessed beautiful people, their wants supplied by a bountiful nature, and mercifully ignorant of the burden of civilization.'

But even by the time of Cook's second visit to Tahiti, some of the ill effects of contact had become apparent. The impact was not yet 'fatal', but the seeds of great harm were already sown. Cook wrote: 'We debauch their morals, already prone to vice, and we introduce among them wants and perhaps diseases which they never before knew, and which serve only to disturb that happy tranquility they and their forefathers had enjoyed.' For, while the Tahitian aristocracy was not at all permissive in sexual matters, the women of the ordinary people were only

Michael Friedel/Rex Features

too friendly to the sailors. Consequently there was a rapid spread of venereal disease which had been unknown until then.

There was also another consequence. Favours once granted freely, had soon to be bought: at first the gift of a nail or two was sufficient, but soon many more were needed and one sailor was flogged for stealing large quantities of ship's nails. And by Cook's third visit the trinkets, which were once so useful, could buy neither food nor favours. The process of commercialization had begun.

By the time of Cook's third voyage another problem was apparent—the Tahitians no longer made their traditional stone tools. Why should they when the Europeans supplied them with better, iron implements? But even at that time the possible consequences of this were realized: soon no-one would know how to make the tools, and what would happen if the supply of European tools ever ceased? Yet Cook knew that the Tahitians could never return 'to the happy mediocrity in which they lived before we discovered them.'

There is an innocence about these early contacts, on both sides, which may make the harm which often resulted hard to criticize. The Spanish sailors who brought the influenza virus to Tahiti can hardly be blamed for the

A rusting tank in the waters of the Caroline Islands is a reminder of the islanders' innocent involvement in the Second World War. The battles between US and Japanese forces left a trail of destruction across many South Pacific islands.

terrible epidemic which resulted, and the enormous number of deaths. It was a cruel accident that the Tahitians had no inherited immunity to diseases which were commonplace and relatively harmless in Europe.

But in the course of the 19th century this innocence entirely disappeared. The development of Western industrial society created a demand for resources—people, as well as land and raw materials—which had a devastating effect on many smaller groups of hitherto isolated peoples. As innocence gave way to greed, unintended harm gave way to systematic exploitation. Whatever advantages Western technology may have brought, nothing could excuse the utter destruction of the way of life and the lives of millions of 'primitive' people throughout the world.

A classic case of colonial viciousness is the treatment of the Tasmanians. The Tasmanians were a people whose technology was undeveloped, even by Australian Aboriginal standards: they did not use fire, they had no houses, pottery or

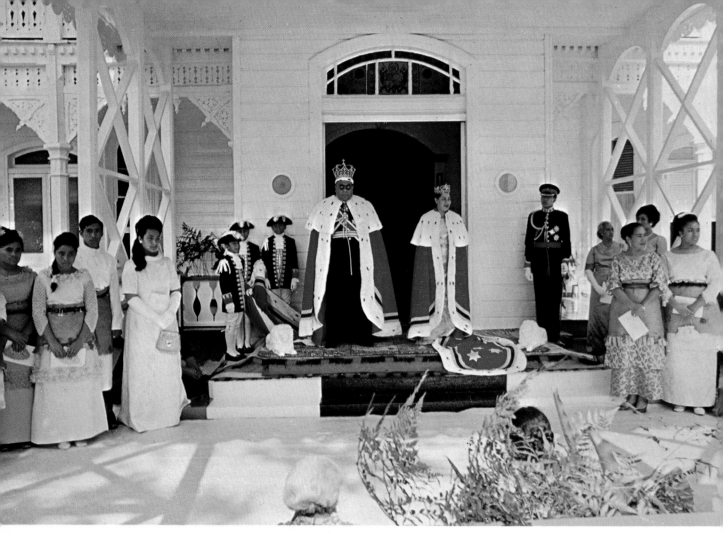

King Tupou IV of Tonga dressed in full Western regalia. The page-boys who attend the queen wear uniforms reminiscent of those worn by British officers of 200 years ago.

domestic animals, and they were ignorant of farming. But they were friendly: Cook remarked on their 'benevolent expression' and thought them generally 'not disagreeable'.

In 1803 a party of European settlers crossed to Tasmania to establish a convict colony. When a group of Tasmanians charged through their camp, in pursuit of wallaby, the commander order his men to fire on them with cannon loaded with grapeshot. Many were killed, and not unnaturally, the Tasmanians later took revenge on a party of whites who also happened to be out getting food: they killed a number of sailors who were gathering oysters. The next quarter of a century saw an 'open season' for hunting Tasmanians: jackets of hunting pink were even worn on occasion.

The law did not protect them—more often it was used to harrass and deprive them more quickly of their lands. Disease killed many, and was even spread deliberately by distributing clothes from infected people in the hope that they too would catch the disease.

The effect of hostility of this kind is obvious: but the situation takes on an air of tragedy when even good motives turn out to have ill effects. A missionary, George Robinson, decided that the only way the few survivors in the 'wild' could avoid total destruction, was if they could all be collected and helped in a mission station which he established on Flinders Island. Every day the Tasmanians were forced to go to church to hear his sermons. But Robinson's version of Christianity, and his naive attempts to teach a form of economics and trade, induced total apathy in the Tasmanians.

The results were soon apparent. Births ceased, and within ten years it was clear that the race was doomed to extinction. The settlement was abandoned, and 47 of the estimated original population of 2,000 Tasmanians returned to the mainland. The 'Tame Mob'—the few who had accepted menial tasks in the town—fared little better. The last pure Tasmanian male died in 1869 and the last woman lies in a coffin in Hobart Museum.

The Tasmanians are an extreme case of such 'final' treatment. Deliberate destruction was rare in the Pacific, although there are parallels in Argentina and other places in South America. But the types of ill effect which destroyed them caused harm over the entire area. Disease has

already been mentioned: smallpox and tuberculosis were the major killers. But the effects of minor diseases can be devastating for those who are not immune, and many thousands of Pacific peoples died from influenza, the common cold, whooping cough, chickenpox and measles. In Fiji an epidemic of measles killed 40,000 people in 1875—one third of the native population.

Social diseases, gonorrhoea and syphilis, spread rapidly in situations where men were forced to live away from their wives. European sailors, soldiers and traders brought death to the Pacific islanders; and generations suffered the long-term effects of venereal disease—declining fertility, a reduced birthrate, and congenital weakness. Only recently has medicine finally managed to overcome the 'fatal impact' of disease, too late to save many thousands of islanders.

In addition to disease, alien customs, morals, laws, and firearms the Europeans brought with them alcohol. The effect of strong Western alcohol on those who were unused to it was severe. A tragic example was the case of King Pomare II of Tahiti, son of the famous Kamahameha. He was described as 'a sad debaucher and a drunkard' and died of chronic alcoholism in 1821. The commander of a Russian ship reported that on one occasion the

For most Pacific islanders, education now takes the form of western style schooling, and little of their traditional culture is taught. These little girls from Fiji wear neat cotton uniforms and sit on benches in front of the blackboard.

John Marmaras/Susan Griggs Agency

Queen herself begged for a bottle of rum.

Alcohol led only too often to despair, violence and psychological dependence. And it was an important contributory factor in the destruction of the social coherence of many Pacific societies.

Societies which have evolved in comparative isolation for a thousand years are apt to be at risk when the isolation finally breaks down. Not surprisingly, matters are generally worse if the society is on the passive end of the contact. For a long time it was thought that the Pacific Islanders were wholly passive in the face of European influences. To a large extent, this was a conceit on the part of the Europeans who chose not to perceive how the islanders often turned matters to their own advantage.

Once European penetration had occurred, change was bound to follow in every 'department' of society. When new ideas of trade and economics are introduced, new political ideas follow inevitably. It is no accident that very soon after the Europeans first arrived, the political systems of Tahiti and Hawaii underwent violent change.

Immediately after Cook's death in 1779 King Kamahameha of Hawaii, father of Pomare II, established a dynasty of unprecedented power which lasted for more than 100 years. His conquest of the formerly independent islands was helped by the use of firearms which he had obtained from the Europeans. New political ideas produced new religious ideas, and made the old ones unacceptable. In Hawaii, for example. King Kamahameha's wife determined that the traditional taboos should go. At a public feast she and other women ate forbidden foods. Kamahameha joined them, and the crowd cried, only too prophetically, 'The gods are a lie.'

The area of breakdown in which the effects were most severe, and most insidious, was psychological. The 'Noble Savage' period was short-lived: it was something of an intellectuals' idea at its most fashionable. The concept had little relevance for the tough traders and soldiers who had most contact with the Pacific islanders in the 19th century, or to

A Bontoc man from the highlands of northern Luzon in the Philippines rests in the shade of a filling station. Most Filipinos have embraced the material culture of the Americans far more thoroughly than the Bontoc tribespeople.

Claus Dieter Brauns

Mary Evans Picture Library

the whalers and planters who followed them. To them the 'native' islanders were savages and altogether inferior people. The tragedy was that the islanders came to believe in their own inferiority.

Missionaries must take a great deal of the blame for this process of psychological 'devaluation'. By teaching that existing ideas of religion were all wrong, and that only they had the truth, they struck deep at the whole system of coherent belief and philosophy which had been current in each society until then. They had, to use one of their own metaphors, introduced guilt into Eden.

Christianity was often far less relevant to the social realities of the islands than existing religions. And its imposition helped to destroy patterns of marriage, prestige and social order. It weakened political authority, and eventually led to the collapse of the entire social fabric. Banning pig-feasting in New Guinea, or forbidding surf riding in Hawaii may seem trivial. But both were essential parts of status-prestige systems, and their decline represented one more crack in the whole social structure.

Hawaii offers an example of what happens in these circumstances. It is true that the original 'Kanaka' population was not actually eliminated, and in this they were more fortunate than the Tasmanians. But their numbers were certainly severely reduced. Cook's estimate of a population of 400,000 was probably exaggerated,

but the next 50 years undoubtedly saw a vast decline. Missionary estimates of 142,000 in 1823 were probably accurate while the census of 1832 gave a figure of 130,000; and that of 1878, 44,000. By 1900 there were only 30,000 native Hawaiians left—less than 10% of the 18th century population.

These numbers were insufficient to supply the demand for labour on the sugar and fruit plantations and many Japanese and other Orientals were brought over: these now constitute the largest part of the population. The native Hawaiians have increased to nearly 90,000, but they are still less than a fifth of the population of 'their' islands. Very little of their culture has survived: a few words like *hula* (hoops) and *luau* (parties) form part of the tourist vocabulary. And customs remain which have proved their value to the 'Visitor Industry'. It is survival, but at a terrible price.

Some Pacific peoples have tried, in a spirit of hostility or violent competition, to get the better of the white master-world, by supernatural means. This led to the development of Cargo Cults in which the leader promised that the products of Western technology would be showered on the cult followers by magical means. But the goods did not come, of course, though the cults have even had revivals in recent times.

Of all the Pacific islanders who have suffered as a result of culture-contact,

While their attention is distracted by local women, British sailors are portrayed as being deftly robbed of their hats and handkerchiefs by Easter Island men. More often, however, it was the islanders who were exploited and abused.

only the Maoris of New Zealand have found a viable solution to the trauma. Like almost all other Pacific peoples, they have suffered greatly at the hands of the Europeans. They have been exploited, and seen their land usurped by invaders. And during the course of the 19th century their population fell to a fifth of its original size.

But they survived. And they achieved this without fruitlessly attempting to ignore the influences of the white world, or allowing themselves to be 'swallowed' by it (like the Hawaiians). The Maoris have taken full advantage of educational opportunities and employment, and have managed to revive an attitude of affirmation, enthusiasm and a creative view of their past—*maoritanga*.

There has been a Maori cultural renaissance, and an increase in population from a low point of 40,000 in 1890 to more than three times that today. It is encouraging that in the case of the Maoris at least, the coming of the Europeans to the Pacific has not meant the death of a culture—the tragedy lies in the uniqueness of this fact. □

Conquest and colonialism

A famous scholar, Dr Victor Purcell, termed South-East Asia 'Indosinesia'. In doing this he meant to emphasize that the origins of the region's cultural roots lay in both India and China. This definition of the region is both accurate and revealing.

The geographical area of South-East Asia—including Thailand, Laos, Cambodia, North and South Vietnam, Malaysia and Indonesia—may be divided broadly into two theatres of influences in historical, pre-Western times.

Indonesia came under Indian influences as waves of different Indian cultures broke on the shores of the archipelago. Those same waves of Indian thought, religion and language also deeply affected Malaya, but not Borneo, Thailand, Laos, and Cambodia.

The region we now call Vietnam, after the fall of the Hinduized Kingdom of Champa in the 15th century, came under strong Chinese influence and part of it was ruled by China from 111 BC to 939 AD. The other parts of the South-East Asian peninsular, especially the coastal regions, also felt Chinese influence in varying degrees, from at least as early as the Tang dynasty (618-906 AD).

But to discover the origins of the peoples of South-East Asia it is necessary to look further back. The similarities between them are not a matter of their physical appearance—for nothing could be more different than the tall, pale-skinned Kenyahs and Kayans of the hills of Sarawak, and the short, dark, rice farmers of central Thailand—but lie in their outlook. An easy-going way of compromising to reach decisions which maddened generations of Dutch, French and British colonial officials and which today reveals itself in the adaptations they have made to democratic forms of government which were at first accepted intact from their former rulers. The most profound and lasting influences have perhaps been from those pre-Western times.

The original inhabitants of South-East Asia seem to have arrived in successive waves from early Neolithic times. The racial composition of the country is extremely mixed because of this and later historical waves of immigrants, a fact that caused Purcell to call the region an 'ethnographic museum.' Java Man flourished in Indonesia in Pleistocene times, over two million years ago. Today's population consists of *homo sapiens* of several distinct types who arrived much later.

Although a trip through Indonesia

The homes of these refugees from Hue were destroyed in the fighting between North and South Vietnam. Although formerly both these countries had come within the orbit of the French colonial empire, in 1954 the North turned to China for aid while the South turned to America.

Bruno ·Barbey—Magnum

Ivan Polunin/Susan Griggs Agency

Fred Mayer/John Hillelson Agency

(Left) The tin-roofed mosque at Sibolga in northern Sumatra. Islam spread throughout South-East Asia, and is still the principal religion among the people of West Malaysia, Sumatra, Java and Borneo.

(Right) This worker in Borneo is coagulating rubber latex with formic acid. Although rubber is less important today than it was at the time of the 'rubber boom' at the end of the 19th century, it still plays an essential part in the economy of South-East Asia.

(Bottom Left) Indonesia was colonized by the Dutch, and initially the wealth from the exploitation of the country's natural resources remained in Dutch hands. Since independence in 1949, however, and the nationalization of foreign assets in the early 1960s, the country has begun to prosper.

(Below) During the Angor period 1,000 years ago, Lesser Vehicle Buddhism, spread from India to many parts of South-East Asia. This Buddhist Temple with a statue of the Indian snake god Naga in the foreground, is in Kampuchea, where there are still more than 5 million adherents.

Bruno Barbey—Magnum

Victor Englebert/Susan Griggs Agency

does not leave an impression of the existence of extremes of human type, even the island of Sumatra contains ethnic types as varied as the broad-headed Mongoloids who came from continental Asia via the great southward running rivers (Mekong, Salween, Red River), and the Caucasoids who are represented by the Batak people.

These human waves from the north brought with them a basic family of languages (later modified by local conditions), a body of beliefs including the idea of a 'god-king', and a material culture which included textiles and bronze-casting.

By the time of the first important Indian and Chinese influences over 2,000 years ago, the civilizations had already separated because of geography and other factors. These then adapted to the influences of Indian and Chinese civiliza-

tions, much in the way that contemporary Europe and the Middle East were adapting to the cultural influence of Greece and later Rome. But the animist and partly pantheist beliefs of South-East Asian societies survived the impact—Hindu insistence on the lowly position of women, to take one example, failed to take root in South-East Asia where women have always held considerable status.

In the early civilizations, prior to the Indian and Chinese impact, were a number of aboriginal peoples who were ethnically dissimilar and represented the descendants of the original inhabitants. Today there are still pigmy Negritos in the mountains of the Malay Peninsula, but they and other aboriginal people now number only a few tens of thousands.

The Negritos were engulfed by the Malays in the Peninsula, just as other tribal peoples were driven into less hos-

pitable parts of their countries by the Cham in central and south Annam, and the Khmer (close relatives of the Mon) in the Mekong River Delta. The Malays spread round the coasts of the Indonesian islands and northern Borneo while the tribal Dayaks inhabited the interior of Borneo.

Today the barriers between South-East Asians are not those of race but of differing culture, and more recently of nationalism. The original formation of states was the natural result of the pressures from the north that made peoples immigrate generally southward. Chinese internal pressures on its minority peoples such as the Thai of south-central China forced them towards Yunnan Province, where a pocket of them still

(Left) Tamil and Chinese rubber tappers carry latex to the local factory in Malaya. The large numbers of rubber workers from India brought Hinduism back to Malaya where long before it had been supplanted by Islam.

The Mansell Collection

Workers on a British rubber plantation in Borneo in the early 20th century. The introduction of rubber from South America made vast fortunes for plantation owners, and provided work for local people.

exists, and later down the rivers to the south. Another movement from south China brought the Annamese into the Vietnamese area. All these movements resulted in the formation of new kingdoms.

The arrival of Indian traders and the founding of Indian trading posts formed foreign coastal colonies in South-East Asia. But two of the earliest empires, Funam and Srivijaya, although Indianized, were actually South-East Asian. We know of them largely from Chinese written sources. Funam started as a nucleus in the southern Indo-Chinese Peninsula, spreading north via the waterways of the Mekong Delta. At its greatest extent it covered present-day Cambodia and the region of Annam, and spread into the Malay Peninsula. From its beginning

in the 2nd century AD, Funam lasted for 500 years: first under the influence of Indian Brahmans, and later the Shiva cult which finally gave way to Buddhism.

Funam's successor, Srivijaya, with its capital at Palembang in south Sumatra, is described by a Chinese pilgrim who arrived there in 672 AD to study Sanskrit before going on to India. It was under this empire that the Buddhist shrine at Borobudur in Java was built. Srivijaya's sovereignty was eventually broken by raiding Cholas from south India. It was succeeded by a usurping Hindu-Javanese culture with the rise of Singosari whose repulse of a Mongol Chinese fleet sent by Kublai Khan laid the foundation of the Modjapahit empire. The era of the great Modjapahit was one of expansion in the 14th century when it controlled the Malay Peninsula and later a large part of the South-East Asian mainland. At its greatest extent, the Moluccas, Borneo and Celebes were also under its control.

Funam's ultimate successor on mainland South-East Asia was the Khmer kingdom, and in 803, Jayavarman II (who came from Java) founded the Angkor kingdom. The Brahman Shivakayvalya became first priest of a new cult of *lingam* worship that was the religion of the Angkor kings. The king himself was a divine personage and the prosperity of the country was thought to be connected to the preservation of the royal *lingam*.

Subduing the Mon to the west, the Khmer also subjected the Cham to the east to their rule in the 12th century. Under the god-king Suryvbarman II, the Khmer took Tonking to the north. In 1177 AD the Cham retaliated and sacked

Angkor. But they were soon expelled and Angkor continued for another two centuries, reaching the height of its glory around 1200 AD.

Meanwhile the Thai, driven from China by the Mongols under Kublai Khan, made themselves independent and overthrew the Khmer, taking Angkor in 1431, and driving them out. Phnom Penh became the Kmer capital (and still is.) The modern state of Kampuchea traces its direct descent, therefore, from Angkor and the Khmer. The first Thai capital was in the north at Chiengmai, and later in the south at Ayuthia.

The Modjapahit empire was assailed by Islam coming from India and from the Moslem conquest of Malacca in 1400, an 'incursion' based on trade, just as Hinduism had been before it.

All these early cultural contacts in Indonesia have left their traces—the Buddhist temple mountain of Borobudur, the curious form of Hinduism that still prevails in Bali, amid a thoroughly Moslem population in the whole of the remainder of the archipelago. On mainland South-East Asia, Buddhism of the Theraveda school still prevails in Thailand, and elsewhere except in the Malay peninsula which is Moslem and in Vietnam where the Buddhism is of the Mahayana variety (from China) and has to contend with the mixture of creeds that constitute Cao Dai, and as well as Taoism and

The Chinese are prominent throughout South-East Asia as merchants, traders and shopkeepers. Their influence is strong in Malaya, and this mine at Ipoh was established by the Chinese to exploit tin deposits.

Catholicism.

This, then, was South-East Asia before the arrival of the first Westerners—the Portuguese. Vasco da Gama was once asked what he sought in the East. He said: 'Spices and Christians'.

The first Portuguese reached Malacca in 1511. It was not long before they were trading there, in Indonesia, and even as far as south China. About a century later the Portuguese were supplanted in South-East Asia by the Dutch, whose desire for spices was every bit as intense, but who did not feel it necessary to proselytize. The Dutch remained in Indonesia, gradually colonizing the whole of the archipelago, until the Japanese drove them from it in the Second World War, and until the Indonesian independence movement finally ousted them as colonialists in 1950.

The only South-East Asian country that was never colonized was Thailand. It has been said that this was because it did not lie on any direct route to China. The feeling of nationality in Thailand was therefore not formed under the yoke of foreign rule, a situation unique in the region. In every other country it was the presence of Western rulers that ignited new nationalist and independence movements.

At first Europeans were in search of spices and other primary products in the East. Later, after the industrial revolution began, they were looking for raw materials, and for places where they could cultivate as well as market their own ever-increasing industrial output. Although the French were fairly successful in what da Gama called his 'search for Christians' (and later urban populations in Indo-China, Cambodia, and Laos had flourishing Catholic communities), the British and Dutch were much less fervent in making converts. Former religious beliefs among the peoples went deeper than Christianity, and elements of local creeds and practices nearly always persisted alongside Christianity in the converts.

The British in Malaya completely altered the appearance and the economy of much of the country by clearing vast tracts of jungle and planting the South American rubber tree. To tap the trees for latex, they brought in very large numbers of Indians as indentured labour. Once more, an element of Hinduism was introduced where it had long ago vanished before the tide of Islam.

The Chinese element in Malaya exploited the many tin deposits, the country's other major resource, and the Chinese

(Left) A Vietnamese woman walks to market. In the background stands the tower of the Catholic Church at Gian-Coc, a reminder of the time when Vietnam was part of the French colonial empire.

(as they have done everywhere else in South-East Asia) became the shopkeepers, the bankers, the money-lenders, as well as determined manual workers and sometimes agriculturalists (such as the pepper-growers of Borneo and Indonesia). Singapore was founded by Sir Stamford Raffles in 1819 at the hub of trade in the East. Dutch outrage at this was finally settled by a treaty of 1824 which outlined the 'spheres of influence' of Britain and the Netherlands in the area.

Borneo was colonized by an Englishman, Sir James Brooke, and ceded to him in return for his pacification of Sarawak on behalf of the Brunei Sultanate. Brunei became a British Protectorate, and North Borneo (now Sabah) was controlled by the British North Borneo Company, much as the East India Company had gradually

Anne de Henning/JohnHillelson Agency

Further war seemed inevitable after the French withdrawal from Vietnam in 1954. This little girl who lost her home in the conflict still wears a protective image of the Virgin Mary around her neck.

colonized India. The task of Brooke in Sarawak, and of the British in Malaya, was at first to pacify warring factions. While Brooke resolutely excluded Christian missionaries, and did little but bring order to his domains, the way of life of the ordinary Malay, Chinese and Indians in Malaya was completely altered by the colonists.

The Dutch in Indonesia introduced the 'Culture System'. Under this instead of giving a proportion of crops, land rents and taxes to the government, the people

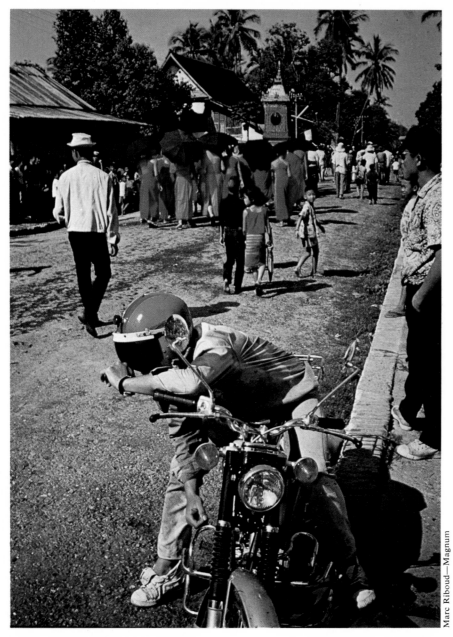

Marc Riboud—Magnum

While monks in Laos gather for a traditional Buddhist ceremony, a motorcyclist starts his machine. Western clothes and consumer goods have become an accepted part of life for the young generation of Indo-China.

had to give up a part of their land, a number of days work and grow specified crops for the government for export. Within 50 years this led to a vast flow of money into the Netherlands' treasury. However it caused not only distress among the Javanese, but also led to widespread corruption. Eventually, it gave way to private capitalist enterprise which tardily began to develop the country's natural resources, and to some extent expanded the economic development of the country.

The French were late arrivals on the scene, but by taking advantage of internal disputes in Annam, and using the murder of a missionary as an excuse, they captured Saigon in 1859. As a result the Annamese Emperor ceded the three eastern provinces to them. Just after this, Cambodia became a French protectorate. The French soon conquered the remainder of the Indo-China peninsula except for Thailand, and learned to rule indirectly through protectorates, local princes and institutions.

Indeed by 1900 the whole of South-East Asia was under Western colonial rule. Only the astute Siamese rulers of the Chakri dynasty held out; they did much to modernize their country, successfully keeping the West at bay while organizing institutions on Western lines.

The Japanese invasion in the Second World War swallowed the whole of the colonial empire in South-East Asia. But with the defeat of the Japanese, the rise of nationalism was soon to throw out the former colonial powers. An Asian people had demonstrated they could throw them out by force of arms, and now the forces of local nationalism proceeded to do the same by various other means.

In 1941 colonialism was superficially intact—20 years later there was almost no remnant of those empires left. The British left Malaya of their own accord and a federation of Malaya, the Borneo territories and, initially, Singapore, became Malaysia. But with commercial power in Chinese hands, and the Malays lagging far behind in both commerce and cultural development (as were the Dayaks), communal friction became at times communal strife. The administrative machinery was, in reality, the most valuable legacy left by the British.

Vietnam, consisting of a northern and a southern rice-growing plain separated by a long, mountainous, and sparsely populated area, was artificially unified by the French; and when they were driven out it reverted to North and South Vietnam. Like the British in Malaya, the French owned nearly all the great rubber estates. French rule was strict, and responsible positions were denied to the Vietnamese élite.

The final French defeat came in 1954 at Dien Bien Phu. But the confusion in the Indo-China peninsula was the direct result of French colonialism with its restrictive measures. The division of Vietnam, and American intervention against the Communist North was another tragic result—for 30 years Vietnam was at war. It can only be said that the outcome of this period of French/American culture contact was disastrous. In spite of the fact that war is no longer a daily reality, its aftermath is difficult, and there are years of recovery to come.

In Indonesia, the consequence of colonial rule may be broadly summed up as an eventual rejection of Western values by the Indonesians. They retained their dependence on the old Moslem faith (in Bali, of course, it was the Hinduized faith) which was combined with even more ancient local spirit worship, and pantheist and animist beliefs. The pattern of democracy has been adapted radically, and through Sukarno's 'guided democracy', its overthrow, and the subsequent rule of the army we see another form of power-weilding. But in its detail it is particularly and characteristically Indonesian or South-East Asian.

Local people gained much higher positions under English rule than under either the French or Dutch administrations. The rift between rulers and ruled was never so deep or so filled with rancour, and the results can now be seen in the healthy relationship that still exists between Britain and her former South-East Asian lands. □

Quest for El Dorado

The history of culture contact in South America began on October 1492 when a small caravelle, the *Santa Maria*, after 10 weeks of uncharted wandering in the Atlantic, anchored off a small island in the Bahamas. The caravelle was part of a fleet of three tiny sailing ships, led by Christopher Colombus, a Genoan by birth, and financed by Ferdinand and Isabel, the King and Queen of Spain.

Many people in Europe, believing the world to be flat, thought the voyagers would end up by going over the waterfall at the world's edge. But Columbus was a proponent of the theory that the world was round and he hoped to reach the Spice Islands of the Indies by sailing west around the globe. The inhabitants were

therefore termed 'Indians'—but this was only one of many delusions that Europeans entertained about the so-called 'New World'.

Colombus was very impressed by his first contact with the indigenous inhabitants of America. 'So tractable, so peaceable, are these people', he reported, 'that I swear to your Majesties there is not in the world a better nation. They love their neighbours as themselves, and their discourse is ever sweet and gentle, and accompanied with a smile; and though it is true that they are naked, yet their manners are decorous and praiseworthy.' But on the day of his arrival, Colombus wrote in the ship's log, 'They should be good servants and very intelligent, for I have observed

that they repeat anything that is said to them and I believe that they would easily be made Christians, for they appear to me to have no religion.' And two days later he observed, 'should your Highnesses command it, all the inhabitants could be taken away to Castille or held as slaves on the island, for with 50 men we could subjugate them and make them do what-

A 17th century German woodcut of the massacre of Indian porters by the soldiers of Pizarro. The impact of the Spanish Conquistadores on the Indians was out of all proportion to their numbers—the mighty Inca empire was conquered by only 180 men.

2615

Victor Englebert/Susan Griggs Agency

(Above) The lost city of Macchu Picchu was the final retreat of the Incas when Cuzco, their royal capital, was destroyed by the Spanish. Undiscovered until 1910, Macchu Picchu is now a major tourist attraction.

(Right) Orlando and Claudio Villas Boas, pioneers in the cause of the Amazon Indians, were the first to contact the Kreen-Akrore tribe. Presents left in the forest were used as a first approach to the Indians who responded by leaving clubs.

Adrian Cowell/Transworld Feature Syndicate

ever we wish.'

Even in that first moment of Colombus' arrival in America, the essential features of the European attitude towards the Amerindians were present—a mixture of idealistic admiration, ruthless material ambition and a desire to convert them to European beliefs. This attitude has moulded relations between Indians and Europeans right up to the present day.

The first stage of European penetration was carried out under the leadership of Spanish soldiers of fortune, many of them minor nobility from the poorer regions of Spain, who hoped to find wealth quickly in America and thereby gain power and distinction within Spanish society. At the time of Pizarro's expedition to Peru in

1532, the central and southern Andes were controlled by the Inca Empire which stretched 4,830km (3,000 miles) from northern Chile to southern Ecuador. Covering an area of approximately 984,200sq.km (380,000 sq. miles) the empire was governed from the capital city, Cuzco, in southern Peru; a network of roads and garrisons similar to that of the Romans in Europe provided firm military control. Inca society was highly stratified, with a sharply defined division of labour. The means of production—the land, the llama herds and the mines—were regarded

as communal property. Furthermore, the Inca state insured people against hunger and privation in old age and times of need by providing them with maize from the central granaries.

The Inca civilization which the Spanish *Conquistadores* encountered was as socially complex as the society from which they themselves came. Nevertheless, it had certain crucial weaknesses which allowed Pizarro, the leader of the Spanish expedition, to gain control of it with a mere 180 soldiers. Firstly, the Incas had neither horses nor firearms and were terrified by

A part-Indian Macumba follower is overcome by a trance. Many Brazilian Indians, now living in towns and cities, have adopted the Macumba, or Voodoo, rituals originally brought from Africa by Negro slaves.

Claus C. Meyer/Colorific!

fined themselves at first to a narrow strip along the East Coast and sought to gain a livelihood from the 'New World' by agriculture, using their own labour or that of African slaves.

The *Conquistadores* did not go to South America with any such desire to build a new society but purely to become rich and powerful within their own lifetimes. The quickest means of doing so was by discovering gold and the *Conquistadores* marched the length of the continent to find it. Although the Spaniards did find many sources of valuable minerals, the fabled city of El Dorado never materialized and so they came to rely increasingly on the labour of the Indians to help exploit the wealth of the continent. In contrast therefore, to the North American Indians, the Indians of South America were forced into the colonial economy from the earliest days.

The treaty of Tordesillas, signed in 1494 between Spain and Portugal, under the aegis of the Pope, established the legal claim—in the eyes of the signatories at least—of the Spanish to all lands more than 370 leagues west of the Azores and Cape Verde Islands. By means of this treaty, the Portuguese had merely hoped to secure their route to India via Cape Horn, but it later gave them title to Brazil, a vast territory that still lay undiscovered in 1494.

The Portuguese colonists confined themselves primarily to the coastal regions, although from the 17th century onwards, they began to settle the banks of the Amazon and its major tributaries. With the exception of some of the missionaries, the first settlers roamed the country in search of wealth, few staying long in any one place. Nevertheless, their presence caused great disruption among the Indians and led to the extinction of the sophisticated Indian cultural groups in the lower reaches of the Amazon. The gradual movement inland of the Brazilian frontier led to a series of Indian wars in the 19th century; but the systematic penetration of the forests of the Amazon, (which comprise some 60 per cent of the land area of the country) did not truly begin until the 1940s when the *Marcha para o Oeste* (March to the West) was launched by President Getulio Vargas.

The 16th and 17th century Spanish conquest quickly led to the enslavement of many Indian peoples. Under the *encomienda* system, the Crown placed control of Indian communities in the

the use of these in warfare. Secondly, Pizarro and his men had a tremendous psychological advantage. Although they were often amazed and terrified by what they encountered, the Spanish at least knew how this contact between two worlds had come about.

The Indians on the other hand had no means of explaining the origin of these strange White men with beards and terrifying weapons of war. They interpreted their arrival as the fulfillment of a myth—a myth encountered among many peoples the world over—that the legend-

ary founders of their own society would one day return.

The motives of the *Conquistadores* who came to plunder were very different from those of the first settlers in North America. Many of the latter were English religious dissidents who crossed the Atlantic hoping to build a new nation where they could be free to practise their beliefs. This difference in motive resulted in completely different patterns of settlement which in turn affected relations between the colonizers and the indigenous inhabitants. The English settlers in North America con-

hands of Spanish landowners who were supposed to protect them and provide them with food and religious instruction. In exchange for these services they were allowed to make the Indians work on their land. As early as the first decade of the 16th century, the ruthless exploitation of Indian labour was denounced by Spanish monks, the most famous of whom was Bartolome de Las Casas, often referred to as the 'Father of the Indians'.

He proclaimed the view—subsequently confirmed by a Papal Bull—that the Indians were rational, endowed at birth with liberty and free will and therefore able to receive the Faith. As a result of the protests of Las Casas and his fellow monks, the New Laws of 1541–1543 were proclaimed by the Crown, abolishing slavery and phasing out *encomiendas*. But the colonists in the New World refused to implement the laws and threatened to rebel. They were unable to share the humanitarian concern of Las Casas.

In 1541, the Bishop of Santa Marta in Colombia felt he should disembarrass the King of the view that the Indians were rational. 'Your Majesty must understand that in these parts, there are no Christians, but only demons . . .' In the face of the threat of rebellion the Crown backed down and the *encomienda* and a modified form of slavery were legalized once again.

The *encomienda* was subsequently replaced by the *repartimiento* system which transferred control of the Indian communities to Crown officials. In theory, the *repartimiento* system should have improved the lot of the Indians since the colonists were now required to pay the Indians a minimum wage. A number of officials, known as *corregidores*, (correctors) were appointed to ensure the Indians were not abused, but such officials thousands of miles from Spain were easily bribed. Most serious of all, the colonists were exempted from their previous obligation to provide their Indian labourers with food.

With the coming of independence to the Spanish colonies in South America during the early 19th century the laws relating to Indian communities were abolished on the grounds that the Indians were now full citizens of their respective republics. Under colonial rule, Indians had been granted legal rights to small areas of land so that they could support themselves. Such rights were held communally and no individual could sell off any portion of the communal land. After independence, this last provision was abolished and the communal lands were divided up amongst the individual members of the community.

Many Indians, inexperienced in matters of property, sold their plots to large landowners for minimal sums. As a result, within a few years, many Indians became vagrant landless labourers and many

sedentary communities were extinguished. In order to keep them on the land that had previously been theirs, the landowners now resorted to a system that had grown up in colonial times. Under debt peonage, which still can be found in many parts of South America today, the *padron* gives the Indians credit in the form of materials such as steel implements, clothes, alcohol and patent medicines at the beginning of a harvesting season. The Indians hope to repay him at the end of the season with part of their harvest. But the *padron* fixes the prices so that the harvest is never quite large enough to pay off the debt and, as a result, the Indians are obliged to return the following season and begin again.

In the gradual imposition of European life on the Indian, missionaries played a crucial role. From that first moment of Colombus' arrival in America, the Europeans sought to convert the Indians to Christianity. There have been examples of individual missionaries who have struggled to protect the Indians from their fellow Europeans; and without doubt many Indian groups in South America were saved from physical extinction only by virtue of such intervention. But these cases are the exception rather than the rule. Backed up by the coercive secular power of the Europeans, the missionaries have forced the Indians to abandon their own customs. Instead they imposed on them a rigid version of European morality, dictating standards in every sphere of life. Forest Indians for example, were obliged to wear clothes in the interest of a prudish sense of decency even though they served little purpose, and led to the outbreak of epidemics as the clothes provided an environment in which viruses could breed.

The missionaries also attempted to settle as many Indians as possible around mission stations. This policy not only made religious indoctrination easier but also allowed the exploitation of Indian labour.

Where both Catholic and Protestant missionaries are at work among the same Indian people, the Indians can sometimes use this to their benefit, playing one off against the other. But it can also have harmful consequences, as in the case of the Tirio who live on the borders of Guyana and Brazil, who have split into antagonistic groups, one nominally Catholic, the other Protestant.

Generally speaking, the Protestants missionaries pose a greater threat than the Catholics to the Indian way of life, being far more ethnocentric and doctrinaire while the Catholics have often been content to impose a thin veneer of Christianity on indigenous religions and beliefs. Protestants, on the other hand, emphasize the need for individual Indians to make a radical break with their past. They must

dissociate themselves from those members of the tribe who refuse to become Christians and strive for personal salvation through the knowledge of Jesus Christ. Failure to do so, they teach, will result in eternal damnation.

Much Protestant missionaryu work goes under the guise of linguistic research. The North American 'Summer Institute of Linguistics', is extremely powerful in South America. The Summer Institute's own publicity material reports that in Ecuador in 1971 its missionaries persuaded the Auca to abandon their territory so that the land could be taken over by foreign oil companies. Thus it is now the Protestants, rather than the Catholics, who form the front line of the European assault on the Indians and their way of life.

The European conquest has been made easier by the epidemics that have ravaged Indian populations ever since the Europeans's first arrival. The Indians had no immunity to the diseases that Europeans brought with them: smallpox, chickenpox, measels, tuberculosis and even the common cold. A calculation of the effect of European diseases on Indians in the early colonial period can only be based on informed guesswork, but in the region of Pamplona in Colombia it is estimated that the indigenous population fell from more than 30,000 at the time of the Spanish Conquest to less than 3,000 at the end of the 18th century.

The Indians interpreted these epidemics as the work of malignant supernatural beings. In the face of the death of half their population many of the survivors appeared to simply lose the will to live and faded away. Many Indians died of hunger rather than of the disease itself because with the whole community confined to their hammocks by illness, there was no-one to go out to search for food. Attempts to treat European diseases by traditional means often made the effects worse. For example, the Indian practice of sitting in rivers to cool the high temperatures that the diseases induced merely made death more likely.

Although recent demographic studies show that if an Indian community does manage to survive the first onslaught of European diseases, it has a strong chance of recovering its numbers, it is a very different society, culturally speaking, that grows out of the ruins of the old.

The reaction of many Indian peoples to the invasion of their lands has been to try and repel the Europeans by force of

Since the 16th century, Indians have been recruited to work in the mines of Peru and Bolivia. Conditions are still very poor and these tin miners chew semi-narcotic coca leaves to numb the effects of cold, altitude and fatigue.

Bruno Barbey-Magnum

(Above) The machinery of conquest—earth-moving equipment at work on the construction of the Trans-Amazon Highway. New roads opening up the forests of the Amazon to Brazilian farmers, ranchers and mining companies will destroy the way of life of many isolated Indian peoples.

(Right) Colorado Indians mingle freely with settlers in the frontier town of Santo Domingo in Ecuador, yet legal and social barriers prevent them achieving equal status with the territory's new inhabitants.

H. W. Silvester/Rapho

arms. The most successful case of armed resistance was that of the Mapuche of Chile. For 350 years, from 1550 until about 1900 when they were finally conquered, the Mapuche held the invaders at bay. But three centuries of warfare brought about major changes in Mapuche society and culture.

Previously a fragmented group with local chiefs, the need to organize resistance led to the emergence of war leaders with authority over the whole group. The Mapuche also evolved a new system of beliefs and cultural practices that stressed their opposition to the Spanish and their values. Anthropologists have argued, for example, that the Mapuche began to practise cannibalism precisely because

they knew that the Spanish abhorred it. Mapuche warriors would ride into battle blowing on trumpets fashioned from the tibia bones of Spanish captives they claimed to have eaten, a strategy that understandably struck terror into the hearts of their adversaries.

In many other parts of the continent Indians have attempted to resist the colonizers by force of arms. In the latter part of the 18th century, Campa Indian rebels seized control of much of southern Peru. They were led by Juan Santos, a *mestizo* who claimed to be a reincarn-

ation of the Inca, Atahualpa. In Argentina the Indians of the Pampas organized themselves into mounted bands to resist the invasion of their territory, but by the end of the 19th century they had almost all died in a series of bitter and merciless wars with the Argentine Army. In Brazil, the Europeans' penetration of the interior of the country has been accompanied by prolonged hostilities. Even today there are frequent reports in Brazilian newspapers of Indian attacks on White outposts. On the other hand the shooting, bombing and even poisoning of Indians

Part-Indian Peruvian soldiers parade the figure of the Virgin Mary through the streets of Ayacucho. The imposition of the Catholic faith went hand in hand with the European colonization of South America.

is considered less newsworthy.

Despite the tenacity with which the Indians may have fought to keep out the invaders, they have eventually had to bow to the superior force of arms of the Europeans. Many Indian groups simply did not realize just how numerous their adversaries really were and thought of the Whites as simply another tribe like themselves. At the beginning of the 20th century, the Kaingang of southern Brazil brought the construction of a railway line through their territory to a halt and the Brazilian authorities, in an attempt to make peace with them, invited their leaders to come to São Pãulo. When the Indians boarded the train that was to take them there they were excited at the prospects of meeting the White chiefs. But as the train progressed towards São Pãulo, and the settlements along the line became larger and larger, the Kaingang became quieter, finally falling completely silent as the horror of the sheer size and complexity of the White world struck home.

Some Indian peoples have thought that the power of the Europeans came from their influence over the supernatural, and so they have tried to gain this influence by adopting the Europeans' religious rituals. The Hallelujah cult of the Akawayo and Patamona of Guyana, for example, is based on a mixture of indigenous and Protestant religious beliefs. Heaven is equated with the traditional notion of a spirit world that existed in the sky. The angels of Protestant mythology are related to the flights that, according to traditional belief, the Indian *shamans*, taking the form of birds, would make to the spirit world. Elements of Protestant ritual such as kneeling and praying, have been incorporated into the traditional Indian religious dancing. As with many messianic movements, the central tenet of the Hallelujah cult is that the Whites have somehow tricked God into giving them the goods and power that rightfully belong to the Indians.

But neither natural nor supernatural means have prevented the gradual erosion of the Indian world. South American

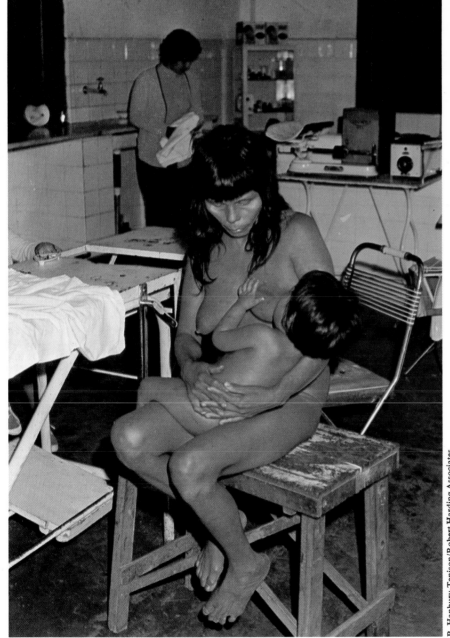

In the Xingu National Park, modern dispensaries like this offer medical help to many of the Indians. However, there is some irony in the fact that many of the diseases which require treatment (and which have wiped out many tribes) were introduced by White people.

Vautier-Decool

R. Hanbury-Tenison/Robert Harding Associates

Reflejo/Susan Griggs Agecoy

A favela shanty-town huddles beneath the statue of Christ on Corcovado in Rio de Janeiro. This is the reality of city life for the thousands of Indians and mestizo peasants who are lured to the urban centres of South America each year.

governments hope that the 'Indian problem' will disappear as the Indians are gradually assimilated into the national society, but the historical evidence indicates that this is by no means an inevitable or a uniform process. Some Indian groups adapt to European habits more readily than others. Some have been in contact with Europeans since earliest colonial days without losing their sense of identity as Indians. This failure, as the Europeans see it, to take up the benefits of civilization is attributed to the 'conservatism' of the Indian. But it is not merely conservatism that is at the root of the 'Indian problem'. The Indians have shown a willingness to adapt to the European way of life where it benefits them, but the role that the national societies offer to the Indian—that of a landless peon, on the very lowest rung of the social hierarchy—is in many cases

worse than the marginal but to some extent self-sufficient life that he already has. In addition, those Indian individuals who do attempt to live like non-Indians are ridiculed and discriminated against by those they attempt to copy.

No matter how wealthy they become many doors will remain closed to them. It is very rare, for example, for an Indian man to marry a non-Indian woman, even though it is relatively common for Indian women to be wives or mistresses to non-Indian men. When an Indian of a tribe in southern Brazil persuaded a Portuguese woman to spend the night in his hut, his fellow Indians drove a stake into the ground to commemorate it.

It is not surprising therefore that the Indians, discriminated against by a society that offers them little or nothing, should value their ethnic identity. But this does not mean that the old ways go on unchanged. The Potiguara of northeastern Brazil, for example, still think of themselves as Indians, even though they have almost entirely abandoned their traditional culture. Instead they affirm their Indian identity in rituals copied from the Negroes of the region.

Since the beginning of the 20th century.

with the foundation of the Indian Protection Service in Brazil, specially appointed government bodies have attempted to administer Indian affairs. Most South American countries have laws or statutes recognizing the rights and needs of Indians. But yet again, theory is far removed from practice. The government bodies are poorly staffed and poorly financed; they are either unable or unwilling to enforce the law. The laws are, in any case, full of loopholes and allow Indian interests to be overridden in the name of a vaguely defined 'national interest'. Thus Indian groups are being chased off their lands as a result of the plans for economic development that are currently being carried out in the Amazon region. The Indians are either directly displaced by road construction or by the immigrants that the roads bring with them. The small, fragmented Indian bands cannot for long resist this influx and retreat further and further into the forest until there is nowhere else to go.

Pioneers in the cause of the Indians of Amazonia, the Villas Boas brothers helped to found the Xingu National Park, only to see it cut in two by a new road. For many years they lived with isolated Indian bands, hoping to prepare them for the coming impact of contact with the outside world. Disillusioned, the brothers announced they were considering abandoning their work a few days after their greatest triumph, in which they finally made contact with the Kreen-Akrore tribe.

The statement they made on that occasion was a stunning indictment of all the attempts of Europeans to save, improve or 'pacify' the Indians of South America.

'We are leaving the life of backwoodsmen because we are convinced that every time we contact a tribe we are contributing to the destruction of the purest things that tribe possesses . . . We never truly reached our objectives. All the "pacified" Indians slowly lose their characteristics and authenticity and their culture is corrupted through contact with civilized outsiders. Once pacified they stop being free and they interrupt the continuation of their cultures. Even if they remain in their natural habitat they are subject to the pressures of civilization.'

This view was vividly confirmed in the televison documentary 'A Decade of Destruction' shown in the U.K. in January 1984. Development continues unabated, and perhaps the only hope lies in the increasing political activity of Indians, directed towards securing their rights within the national community. Colonization may have weakened tribal identity but it has also strengthened ethnic consciousness, giving all Indians a common cause since they have a common oppressor. □

The sleeping dragon

As early as 3,000 years ago, there emerged in China a Bronze Age whose ritual vessels remain unsurpassed as objects of technological perfection and beauty. We may take this period as an example of Chinese culture in its earliest definable times, and with it place the invention of Chinese ideographic script which appears to have grown up at the same time. Already, in the great age of bronze, that script had graduated from mere pictograms representing objects, to the invention of ideograms expressing concepts.

By the time of Christ, China had been unified as a homogeneous cultural mass for about two centuries. Since then it has remained the largest and most populous geographical area in the world, a culture expressed in one written language and in one basic system of philosophy underlying both government and morality.

China has always consisted of a compact populated area, whose southern and eastern boundaries were the Pacific Ocean, while its neighbours to the south, south-west and west have for the most part been physically separated from the Chinese by mountain ranges, some of formidable height, and having few passes. To the northwest and north, deserts and more mountains formed natural barriers through which corridors of communication were few and arduous. For this reason it is hardly surprising that Chinese history reveals long periods of isolationism and xenophobia.

China's immediate neighbours on all its landward boundaries were demonstrably less culturally advanced, and this fact tended to confirm the Chinese in their conviction that Chung Kuo—the Central Country, as they name their land—had the only worthwhile civilization in the world. The vast enclave of China was ruled by dynasties of emperors wielding absolute power, but in general applying it lightly to governors and

Completed during the reign of Shih-Huang-ti in the 3rd century BC, and stretching 2,710km (1,684 miles) from the Gulf of Pohai to Chiayukuan, The Great Wall of China is the greatest construction project ever undertaken. The wall was built as a barrier in the north, but did not prevent the Mongol invasion in the 13th century AD.

Bruno Barbey/Magnum

These massive Buddhist statues are carved out of the solid rock in the Yukan caves. Buddhism—together with Zoroastrianism and Nestorian Christianity—was very influential during the T'ang dynasty, until official edicts denounced the religions as un-Chinese.

viceroys of the provinces who actually controlled regional and temporal affairs.

Internally, China was self-sufficient in most respects. It grew enough rice and other crops to feed her population, although as the population became more numerous there was increasing hardship and hunger when the vagaries of the climate—the flooding of great rivers, and recurrent droughts—affected a people whose reserves were always small. When needed, food was hard to distribute because of the inadequacy of the communication network. But on the whole the Chinese felt themselves to be a superior, self-sufficient people. The Ch'ien-lung Emperor in the late 18th century felt able to write with utter (if ill-founded) conviction, in reply to a letter from George III of England, that China 'possesses all things' and had no need of the West's manufactures. It was close to the truth. What China needed from the outer world had always been obtained from Arab trading-boats and from the various surrounding peoples who brought such goods as furs, jade, minerals, spices, birds' nests and other edible exotica, as their annual 'tribute' to the Son of Heaven at the capital at Peking and by way of barter trade.

In the light of China's physical and intellectual isolation it is perhaps surprising to discover that in the 2,000 years of its dynastic history there have been periods when the country was very open to the ideas and techniques of one or other part of the outer (and by its definition, barbarian) world.

The first of these outward-looking periods came in the T'ang dynasty (618–916 AD) when all roads—not only those of China itself, which were already highly developed, but of Asia in general—led to the capital at Ch'ang-an near the middle Yellow River. At this time camel caravans crossed and re-crossed the great desert and steppeland heart of Asia as they had done sporadically since the days of the Roman Empire when the silks of the Seres (as the Chinese were named then) caused a dangerous outflow of precious metal currency from the Roman treasuries.

In the T'ang period, silk was still a prized commodity in those parts of the West that could afford it. But it is probable that the main trade went towards China rather than the other way. The silver vessels of the Sassanians and many

(Below) This 19th century engraving shows the English missionary James Legge. Although Legge, and others like him, exerted a generally benign influence, the perversion of Christian principles was one of the factors which led to the T'aip'ing rebellion of the 1850s in which more than 20 million people died.

Bruno Barbey/Magnum

John Hillelson Collection

(Above) English, French, German and Japanese officers and their men photographed in Shanghai in 1900. After the failure of the Boxer rebellion—whose slogan was 'down with the Manchu dynasty and drive the foreigners into the sea'—China was divided up between the great Western powers and Japan.

Mary Evans Picture Library

other luxury articles from Middle Eastern lands came in quantities to China, as did multitudes of foreign people to be employed as barbers, grooms, servants, dancers, acrobats and musicians in the noble households of Ch'ang-an and elsewhere in China.

In the 1st century AD Buddhism had arrived from India, but it was not until the T'ang dynasty that it reached its fullest Chinese development, along with Zoroastrianism and Christianity in its Nestorian form from Syria. All three were eventually cut down to size by edicts dissolving their huge establishments as being contrary to the purity of the essential Chinese way of life that was regulated by a form of state Confucianism.

But the process was reciprocal, and many Chinese ideas were transmitted to the rest of Asia. There were Chinese Buddhist monks wandering in India for decades in search of the true *sutras* (or written religious material) of Buddhism, and returning to consult with Indian Buddhist priests in the monasteries of the capital. Buddhism deeply affected both the indigenous Taoism and Confucianism.

At the end of the T'ang period, China fragmented into several states, some ruled by neighbouring peoples, and was not re-unified until the Sung dynasty in 960 AD. After these foreign incursions, China once again turned inwards. The influences of the outside world had been completely assimilated, and a period of intense 'Chineseness' followed. During the Sung dynasty, what was perhaps the great peak of Chinese civilization was reached. No greater masterpieces of painting,

porcelain or calligraphy were achieved, even in the brilliant centuries that followed.

The ethnic explosion of the Mongol peoples in the 13th century took these nomads to the borders of what is now Germany in the west, and to the Pacific Ocean in the east. All China fell to them, piece by piece, under the rule of Kublai Khan. For a century China was again open to the outside world, through the Mongol-controlled trade routes across Asia, and also by sea. The West came to China again in the persons of thousands of traders—such as the Venetian merchant Marco Polo and his father and uncle—and slightly later missionaries such as the saintly John of Montecorvino. It was Montecorvino who set up the first Christian Church in Peking, which had become the capital of China. He was later made the first archbishop of the city by the Pope far away in Rome. Yet the Chinese took surprisingly little from this century of foreign rule (perhaps because they so hated their Mongol rulers), and Christianity died out with the retreat of the invaders, leaving nothing behind it.

With the end of Mongol rule and the reinstatement of a Chinese dynasty with the august Ming, there followed another period of isolation and dislike of foreigners. China closed her frontiers and forbade her people to leave the country; all foreigners were expelled. With the exception of minimal trading which carried on as it always had at South China ports (where colonies of Arabs and other traders seem to have lived in peace with the Chinese), China was a closed land.

Spices, various exotic medicines and foods were imported from India, Indonesia and elsewhere in the Nan Yang—the Southern Seas. The Middle Eastern cobalt, which was superior to the Chinese mineral for painting the blue on porcelain, was also collected and transported by Arab ships.

There was one exception to this isolationalism: the voyages of the Chinese eunuch Admiral Cheng Ho. His huge ships, each with several hundred men aboard, sailed to the Indonesian archipelago, Malaysia, Ceylon, India and reached the eastern shores of Africa, returning with such exotica as peacocks, giraffes, gems and even petty kings. The purpose of the voyages seems to have been to set up and to strengthen existing trading stations. But they did not continue for long, and there was no colonization.

Since the T'ang period at least, Chinese traders had lived in various parts of South-East Asia, often dominating the local economy, yet they never appear to have had the desire to annexe the countries. The acquisition and loss of territories adjacent to China itself, which went on over the centuries, was largely defensive in character. It was aimed both to create buffer-zones, and a means by which trade routes could be protected, and finally it was aimed at the pacification of belligerent tributary states.

At the end of the Ming dynasty, the first Jesuit to enter China, Matteo Ricci, penetrated south China and gradually worked his way up to Beijing (Peking) where he established himself and other Jesuits with a church in the capital. He only succeeded in doing this by his extraordinary skill in speaking and writing Chinese, and by his scientific achievements which were of interest to his hosts.

Ricci was followed by many other European Jesuits, including several outstanding scholars in mathematics and astronomy—learned men well equipped to represent all that was best in the Western civilization of their times. But neither Christianity, nor Western scientific achievements which were now in advance of those of China, made any lasting or deep impression on Chinese life and thought. Christianity was reviled and cast out, and its priests kept on by successive emperors as tame artisans and painters in the palaces. China, superior and condescending, continued with her traditional isolation, dealing with the outside world only on its own terms.

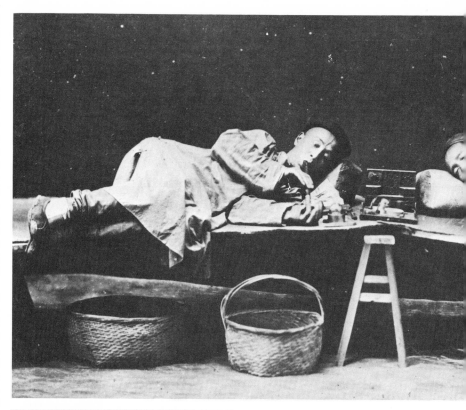

Tea workers in Canton in 1870 carry out the infinitely tedious process of rolling a bag of ho-ting leaf into round balls. The opening-up of trade with the West made enormous demands on the domestic industry, resulting in rapid expansion.

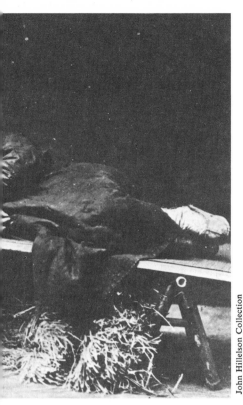

(Above) An 1875 photograph of opium smokers. The British East India Company effectively created wholesale addiction in China, by exchanging opium for tea.

(Below) An Englishman presides over a traditional Chinese magistrate's Court. The Treaty of Tientsin in 1860 permitted Western powers to penetrate deep into China, each establishing its own sphere of influence.

Various embassies—from Russia, from the Dutch, who were established in the East Indies, and from Britain—were treated in rather the same fashion as the tribute missions sent by adjacent countries on an annual or bi-annual basis. Their claims to equality with China and their desire to trade and to set up permanent commercial or diplomatic missions in China were all rejected. The exception was Russia. Considered a potentially powerful neighbour, Russia's frontier marched with that of China and was adjusted by the first treaty China ever signed with a Western power, the treaty of Nerchinsk in 1689.

China, living in splendid isolation, continued in her ancient ways until the rise of industrial Britain in the 18th century. The expansionist tendencies of Britain, and the need to find sources of raw materials to feed her ever-growing industrial machine, and to discover outlets for its products, had already resulted in the subjection of India. The British also believed that they had the *right* to trade. To the Chinese, no such idea existed. Merchants, along with such people as actors and soldiers, belonged to the lowest of the four strata of society. The elements of capitalism had hardly entered Chinese life, which was still ruled in a semi-feudal, Confucian manner. The advent of the West in the form of merchant-adventurers in large and heavily armed ships was the most extraordinary event. It was also the harbinger of the most profound cultural shock that China had ever suffered.

By the time of Lord Macartney's embassy in 1793—sent by the British Parliament and bearing a letter from King George III to the Ch'ien-lung Emperor of China—the Chinese were trading regularly with the British, Portuguese and others at Canton in south China. Seeing the determination of the West to buy tea and porcelain, silk, medicinal herbs and plants such as rhubarb, and other goods, China had been gradually edged into foreign trade on a limited basis with people whom she regarded as barbarians. Indeed, the behaviour of the foreign traders often substantiated this opinion. In his reply to George III, the Emperor had pointed out, more or less accurately, that China was self-sufficient. And indeed the great merchantmen of the East India Company arrived in Canton from India with their holds mostly loaded with ballast. There was little that China would buy from the industries of the West. Woollen cloth woven in England was one small item that found a ready sale, but there was little else.

The result of this was that silver, the only currency accepted in China, rapidly drained out of the Western coffers to pay for the staggering amounts of tea that were now being bought in China and drunk in the West. The solution to this imbalance of trade was eventually found in opium. This was grown in India and exported to China in vast quantities.

No-one knows why opium found such a ready market in China, but once the fact was discovered, the East India Company forcibly put vast areas in eastern India under the opium poppy, and the drug (although technically not carried in the company's own ships) was sold to others to be transported to China.

Opium was an illegal import in China. Many imperial edicts made this clear, although it had been grown on a small scale for hundreds of years in the country and used as a medicine just as it was in England. The massive smuggling into China via a network of Chinese spies and venal missionaries who were in the pay of merchants and spoke Chinese, gradually altered the whole economy of south China. Silver quickly drained out of the country, great fortunes were made by Chinese officials who were paid to turn a blind eye to the nefarious activities of the Western merchants and their Chinese 'running dogs'. The already weak Manchu dynasty was further weakened as the corruption spread upward to those in highest office who had also to be rewarded for not knowing what was going on.

When matters reached a head in the third decade of the 19th century, the Emperor sent a high official, Commissioner Lin, to Canton to put a stop to opium smuggling. The story that followed is something like that of the Boston Tea Party. Lin ordered vast quantities of opium to be surrendered, confined the merchants to their Canton factories, and tried to make them sign documents promising never to import it

again. When they would not, he burned the opium.

Shortly afterwards, Britain went to war with China—the First Opium War of 1839–42. With superior armaments and warships, Britain won, and China was forced to sign the first of what the Chinese call the Unequal Treaties (since they were signed at gunpoint). By this treaty Britain annexed Hong Kong, gained the right to trade at other ports in China besides Canton, to appoint consuls at these ports who would deal on equal terms with Chinese authorities, and to be treated according to British not Chinese law. The treaty also stipulated that rights gained by other nations in China would automatically be offered to Britain. A tariff was fixed on all goods imported, and the Chinese were forced to pay not only the costs of a war they had not started, but also to indemnify the merchants for the illegally imported opium they had quite legally burned.

The Treaty of Nanking spelled out all too clearly the pattern of future relationships between China and the West for the ensuing hundred years until at last China regained her sovereignty. Two reactions of that time, coming from highly placed and responsible men, summed up the situation. Gladstone, a young man in the British House of Commons, replied to the Foreign Secretary, Palmerston, that 'a war more unjust in its origins . . . more calculated to cover this country with permanent disgrace, I do not know . . .' And the astute Governor-General of a Chinese province remarked that his country's defeat was the result of 'our military affairs being in the hands of civil officials, who are very likely admirable calligraphists but know nothing of war.'

The civilization of China was, in all but very recent technological developments, at least equal to that of Britain and Europe. And, as a tiny handful of men on both sides recognized, it was in this matter of technology that the dangers lay. It took another war begun by Britain (the Second Opium War of 1860) after which even further concessions and vast sums of money were wrung from China, to put China in Western chains. The deepest impact of the outside world on China was the superior force that it could apply. It is hardly surprising that the Chinese regarded what they learned of Western culture as being akin to a phil-

Female troops in Mao's army parade through the streets during the 1946–1949 civil war. Although disastrous contacts with the West in the past have tended to increase China's traditional isolationism, ironically it was a Western political ideology—Communism—which ultimately transformed Chinese society.

Henri Cartier-Bresson/Magnum

osophy that placed guns and soldiers and traders first, and real 'culture' far behind.

China was now wide-open to Western trade. The Treaty of Tientsin in 1860 extracted the usual massive indemnity in silver, but more importantly permitted Britain and other Western nations to penetrate deep into China. Britain and France, who had occupied Peking and forced ratification of the treaty, established their 'spheres of influence', as did various other nations.

In the treaty there was also a 'most favoured nation clause' which meant that what China granted to one nation she must automatically grant to another. It was not long before, in terms of trade and influence, China was virtually parcelled out among the European nations. Only the jealousy between Western nations and their own shifting alliances prevented the colonization of China in the way that Africa had been colonized and divided up.

Large numbers of Westerners now resided in the coastal cities, and ever-growing numbers of missionaries worked in the countryside. For the first time the Chinese were exposed in large numbers to Western 'culture'. One part of the culture they discovered was purveyed by commercial enterprises, most of which were concerned solely with making as much money as quickly as possible out of China and the Chinese. The human misery of Shanghai, a city created by Western business, can hardly have been equalled even in the new manufacturing cities of Britain during the worst days of the industrial revolution.

The other side of the Western cultural coin was presented by Christianity and its priests. Early 19th century missionaries—like the American Dr Peter Parker with his highly successful hospital at Canton, or men such as the Englishman James Legge—exerted an influence that was largely benign and demonstrated a sincerity that was not lost on those Chinese who came into contact with it. But most priests of all denominations tended to disrupt the pattern of Chinese life. Their converts, in a country as poor as China, were mostly 'rice Christians'— a privileged group looked after by the priests whose activities were, by treaty, protected by the government of China. Thus the government was seen to uphold the privilege of a few Chinese against their fellows, often with no reason. Anti-government sentiments due to this, and to the fact that foreigners were judged by their own and not China's laws (and took gross advantage of it), had the effect of weakening the power of the Manchu rulers, and even of local magistrates deep in the country.

Chinese sentiments may be judged by the spate of cartoons that appeared in China in the latter half of the 19th century. In many of these, Christ is depicted as a

pig hung on a cross, worshipped by stupid Chinese, while the foreigners are raping Chinese women.

One of the most serious consequences of Christian influence was the T'aip'ing Rebellion which broke out in the southern provinces, and raged from 1850 to 1864. The T'aip'ing leader was a Chinese who based his activities on a version of Christianity he had picked up from various Western missionary sources. The rebellion and its suppression, in which the Victorian hero Charles Gordon played a part, cost at least 20 million lives and untold misery in south and central China, and all but toppled the dynasty.

The causes of the rebellion were, of course, partly the terrible state of the Chinese economy, and not merely the perversion of Christian principles held by the T'aip'ing leaders. But in turn, the degenerating economy of China was partly the result of the commercial rape of the country by foreigners. The economy of whole provinces could be turned upside-down by the massive introduction of cheap Western cotton cloth, putting millions of people out of work and altering every detail of the ancient

Silk workers sort larvae in a factory near Shanghai. In the early 20th century imported Western industrial techniques and the abundance of cheap labour brought conditions reminiscent of the worst horrors of the English Industrial Revolution to many Chinese towns.

Chinese rural economy.

The popular Chinese reaction was crystallized in movements that are typified by the so-called Boxer Rebellion of 1900. The Boxers slogan was: 'down with the Manchu dynasty, and drive the foreigners into the sea'. Later, the anti-Manchu part was dropped. The Manchu and Boxer seige of the legations in Peking, and its failure, resulted in the final domination of China by the Western powers who had by then been joined by Japan.

Several decades prior to this, Chinese intellectuals had made a slow, confused attempt at reforms called the 'self-strengthening movement'. It was gradually realized that without foreign technology, and an entirely new way of governing the country, China could never hope to resist

Emil Schulthes/Transworld

The industrial town of Han-yang on the River Han where it joins the Yangtze-Kiang. Resistance from the Empress Dowager early in the 20th century could not lessen the impact of Western capitalism on China, and by the 1920s towns like Han-yang were growing up around rapidly expanding industries.

the inroads of Western business, and the destruction of Chinese values. The young and idealistic Emperor, influenced by a small group of progressive officials, issued decrees outlining sweeping reforms. This period in 1898, called the 'Hundred Days' ended by the usurping of power by the Empress Dowager, the evil genius of Imperial China's last decades. The reform decrees were rescinded and the Emperor kept a virtual prisoner.

But the reforms themselves, and the reformers, clearly indicated the deep influence of Western culture on the intelligent Chinese mind. After the defeat of the Boxers in 1900, and the occupation of Peking by the Western allies, no-one, not even the Empress Dowager, could stem the tide of anti-dynastic feeling. This

was based on internal chaos—itself in part due to the impact of Western capitalism on an economy in which capitalism had previously shown few signs of life.

China, now dismembered into 'spheres of influence' each belonging to one or other Western power, was temporarily pulled together under the influence of a Western-trained doctor, Sun Yat-sen. His republic lacked the armed force to make it work, and China slid into warlord strife. The situation finally erupted into civil war after the defeat of the occupying Japanese in the Second World War.

China was divided between the Nationalists—led by Chiang Kai-shek and backed by Chinese bankers, industrialists and the Western powers—and the Communists under the leadership of Mao Tse-tung and supported largely by the rural Chinese peasants. In 1949, after four years of civil war, Peking finally fell to the Communists. The Nationalists were driven into the sea, and out to Formosa. So too was the West and its ideas. Ironically, the Communist ideology that now dominated China, was itself derived from the west.

But finally, as the world now realizes,

Chinese Communism is proving a vastly different thing from Western Communism. It has been transfomed by the Chinese into a Chinese way of life. Yet there can be no doubt that despite the almost always disastrous effect of Western culture (or at least of that part of it which was conveyed to China) it was a Western political system, imported Communism, that finally vanquished China's outmoded dynastic system.

But there can also be no doubt that, in the future, the system will become so Chinese that we will have to call it by its other name, Maoism—because the genius of the Chinese people will have made it uniquely their own. Similarly far back in the T'ang period, it will be recalled that Indian Buddhism was made Chinese, and Sassanian silver designs became marvels of Chinese porcelain.

The cultural impact of the outside world on China has now come full circle and the Chinese have rejected most of it. What they have taken, they are transforming out of all recognition. All that remains of the centuries of contact with other peoples is a growing Western-style technology, and a Western ideology that will soon be as Chinese as its calligraphy. □

The land of the Aborigines

Most people tend to think of the Australian Aborigines as isolated desert-dwelling people who had no contact with the outside world until the British founded a colony at Port Jackson in 1788. But in fact there had been earlier contact between the Torres Strait Islanders and a number of Cape York Peninsula tribes in Northern Queensland; and between Malays and many Arnhem Land tribes in the Northern Territory. Matthew Flinders, in 1802, was the first European to discover the existence of Malay contact. It seems that Malays had been visiting Northern Australia for about 200 years. They came from Macassar and crossed the Arafura Sea, generally arriving at the Arnhem Land coast just before the rainy season at the end of the year. Normally they stayed for a few months and returned with the trade winds.

Judging from the evidence of shipwrecks which Flinders found on Bentinck Island and the Pellew Islands, the voyage was not without its dangers. The object of the Malays' expeditions, which according to Flinders involved about 60 ships and 1,000 men, was trade. The Malays were eager to obtain *bêches-de-mer*, or trepang. In exchange for *bêches-de-mer* and other goods, the Malays traded dugout canoes, iron axes, knives, pipes, cloth, rice, tobacco and gin with the Aborigines. This form of exchange fitted in well with the traditional Aboriginal way of exchanging goods, for throughout Australia there was a large network of exchange linking many tribes; products from the coastal tribes would eventually make their way far inland. So the Malays, in a sense, were just one more tribe for the northern coastal Aborigines to trade with.

The Malays influenced the material culture and social life of many coastal tribes. Before their arrival, the usual form of water transport was the bark canoe. Although these canoes were fragile and did not last very long, they were easily made and could be readily replaced. The Malays introduced dugout canoes and since these were more stable and made travelling easier, their use by the Aborigines soon became common. Although the

Government settlements and Christian missions like this one have been set up all over Australia to help the Aborigines adjust to the invasion of Western civilization. However, their success has been limited, since they tend to merely maintain the Aborigines' precarious position on the fringes of White society.

David Moore/Transworld Feature Syndicate

Mansell Collection

Aborigines also took up the use of mast-poles and pandanus sails, few bothered to build outriggers. The Aborigines bene-fitted from the use of these canoes since it made their hunting of dugong (sea cows) and turtles more efficient. More efficient hunting meant more turtle and tortoise shells for trading with the Malays; these shells were of no value to the Aborigines, they were merely a by-product of their hunt for meat. In exchange, iron axes and knives were given to the Aborigines.

It is unlikely that tobacco was first

(Left) Embittered convicts from coastal settlements were often the first Europeans to contact many eastern Aborigine tribes The Whites often maltreated the indi-genous people and introduced diseases such as smallpox and measles which decimated their numbers.

(Below) The explorer John Batman 'purchases' 242,800ha (600,000 acres) of land near Geelong and Mel-bourne from a local Aboriginal tribe in 1836. To the Whites in Australia land has always been a commercial commodity; to the Aborigines it embodies everything—their home, their livelihood and their religion.

Australian News and Information Bureau

introduced by the Malays, for there were some mild tobacco plants which the Aborigines used to roll in ashes and chew, but it is possible that the Malays taught them how to smoke. There is certainly no doubt that the bamboo pipe, which is still common in northern Australia, has its origin in Malaya. It consists of a hollow piece of bamboo or cane with a hole on the side near the distal end; this hole is often lined with tin and so forms the bowl of the pipe.

Malay influence can also be detected in some Aboriginal personal names and place names. At one time there was a Malay pidgin which became a *lingua franca* for the northern coastal tribes. The dugout canoes made visiting easier for distant tribes and having a common vocabulary made it easier to communicate. Malay influence can also be seen in the social life of the Aborigines, particularly in some of their religious rites. The Murngin tribe, for example, have incorporated the Malay mast-lifting ritual into their funeral ceremonies. When the Malays were preparing to depart for home at the end of their sea trading expeditions, they would place the mast-pole into position while praying for a safe journey. The Murngin used this act as a symbol to indicate that the soul of a dead person had departed from this world. When the body was placed in the grave the Murngin would chant a prayer in pidgin Malay so that the spirit would have a safe journey. A mast raised over the grave acted as a gravestone.

The Malays never settled in Australia and it is unlikely that they ever intended to do so. They came without their wives and children and apparently they seldom had anything to do with Aboriginal women. Mixed parentage of Malay and Aborigine is quite unusual. On the whole the Malays left the Aborigines to themselves and only came into contact with them on trade matters. For the most part they lived on board their boats or built rough shelters on shore. Archaeological excavations have found evidence of structures with low stone walls which may have been temporary shelters or places for cooking the *bêches-de-mer*.

The Malays did not attempt to teach the Aborigines about their own religion—Islam—nor about farming or any of the arts of their civilization. They enjoyed a good reputation with the Aborigines who claimed that the Malays, unlike the Europeans and Japanese, left their women alone. The tribal structure of the Aborigines remained unaltered by this foreign influence. The only reason why the trading relationship with the Malays has not continued to this day is because the Australian Government was asked to intervene. European pearlers complained that when they had established a trade for pearls with the local Aborigines, the

Roxby Press/British Museum

This pictorial proclamation was issued to the Aborigines by Governor Davey in 1816. But claims to equality of treatment have largely been fictitious. Although over the last 20 years Aboriginal rights have been supported by State governments, most Aborigines still suffer from a poor education, badly paid jobs and often appalling living conditions.

divers would transfer their business to the Malays as soon as they appeared. This White Australian policy of keeping Malay traders out of Australian waters, and not allowing the Aborigines the choice of trade outlets, persisted for a long time.

Nowadays the only evidence that the Malays visited Northern Australia is seen in the use of dugout canoes among some tribes, bamboo pipes, some Malay words, certain features of Aboriginal rituals and the presence of tamarind trees which the Malays undoubtedly planted.

How different the influence of Europeans has been! While the Malays left the tribes more or less as they found them, even though they had been in regular contact with them for at least two centuries, the Europeans completely destroyed many tribes in a few decades. Of those tribes that have managed to survive to the present day, most have had their local and social organization drastically changed. They can now hardly call their land, on which they had lived for centuries before the advent of the Europeans, their own. And it is this matter of land which is the crux of the 'Aboriginal problem'.

While the Malays went to trade, the British went to settle and to take over the land for farming, to graze their stock, to mine the minerals and to cut the timber. In many places the Aborigines, or what was left of them, were herded on to

David Moore/Colorific!

among them.

How did all this happen? Why has there been such a difference in what happened to the Aborigines during contact with the Malays and later with the British? It cannot be explained simply on the basis that the British are evil while the Malays are not, though the Aborigines may, with some justification, think so. Indeed, not surprisingly, many Aborigines today have a rather low opinion of White people and look upon them as being exceptionally greedy and always after something in exchange for a lot of hum-bug. The Malays, on the other hand, had something useful to give in exchange. The relationship between the Aborigines and the Malays was a one-to-one relationship.

(Left) At Amoonguna mission, in Central Australia, an Aborigine learns to use a lathe. Having machine shops and other training centres in mission communities helps the Aborigines learn the skills which are necessary for well-paid employment in modern Australia.

(Right) Deprived of their land and caught between their own traditional values and the standards of Western society, many Aborigines cannot resolve the conflict. They become destitute, often living in desperate conditions on the outskirts of small country towns.

(Below) Many remote desert Aborigines prefer a traditional lifestyle, but they often need help from their local mission when times are hard. Here a truck from Warburton Mission in Western Australia distributes food to the local people.

government settlements and missions on land that was usually poor, or was not immediately wanted by the settlers. The Aboriginal population dropped dramatically from about 300,000 to 70,000 and perhaps even much less. There are many instances of Aborigines being hunted down as if they were vermin. They were killed by punitive expeditions in order 'to teach them a lesson'. There were cases when they were given sacks of flour which contained arsenic. Often when a section of land was taken over as a sheep run, the local Aborigines were forbidden to hunt on that land, even though it still belonged to their tribe. Even nowadays when the land of the few remaining tribes is found to be rich in some mineral, such as bauxite, their rights are practically ignored.

In the past, the Aborigines had a complex religion of their own, yet nowadays one finds Catholics, Presbyterians, Lutherans, Methodists, Seventh Day Adventists, Anglicans and other sects

R. A. Gould

Perhaps the Aborigines did not always get the best of the exchange with the Malays, but they did not end up any poorer afterwards and they usually came away with something substantial. Furthermore the Malays had no intention of settling in Australia and they did not attempt to dispossess the Aborigines of their land.

The British were initially interested in trading but quickly discovered that the Aborigines had few trade goods that they wanted. However, the Aborigines did have one important thing—land. But land was not a marketable commodity among the Aborigines—it was inalienable, for it was life itself and formed the basis of everything including their religion. Land was not something that was traded, sold, or gained by force.

Unlike Europeans, Aborigines considered that one was a citizen in a particular place because one was conceived there and not just because one was born there; thus it was possible to have rights in more than one area. The Aborigines certainly appreciated the economic importance of land, but they have always regarded it as much more than an economic good. But to the British settlers land was a marketable commodity which could be bought and sold and had nothing to do with religion.

At the end of the 18th century the British had to find somewhere other than America to send their convicts. It was decided to set up a colony at Botany Bay where it was hoped that the prisoners would be turned into useful citizens. At the same time this would hinder any designs that the French might have had in settling there. It was the very permanency of the British settlers which irreversibly changed the Aboriginal social organization.

In the first year of the new European colony it was touch and go whether it would be able to survive. The hot sun seemed to scorch the life out of anything that was planted. Phillip, the first Governor, was prepared to be friendly with the Aborigines. Indeed, soon after the colony was founded, he actively sought their friendship in the hope that they could give him information about the local resources. But soon there was conflict when the Aborigines attempted to help themselves to some of the fish caught by the settlers or when they defended their women from the advances of some of the convicts.

When the Aborigines killed one of Phillip's hunting servants, who had a reputation as a vicious man and had probably shot some Aborigines in the bush, Phillips arranged the first 'punitive expedition'. In revenge he was determined to have the heads of 10 Aborigines. The expedition went tramping off into the bush armed with axes to chop off the heads, and sacks to put them in. Not surprisingly the expedition ended in a complete fiasco, with the Aborigines fading off into the trees.

The Aborigines kept so much to themselves that Phillip at one point kidnapped two or three of them in the hopes of gaining information about the country and so that the Aborigines would learn about the good life of the settlers. But these captives either died or escaped. There was another side of the picture. The Aborigines could not understand why the convicts were so brutally treated. Since many of the convicts were from the slums of London and had been imprisoned in rotting ships for a long time, they were scarcely in a physical condition to make their living from the soil in a strange country. They were hardened men and women who had been treated badly and no doubt some of them treated the Aborigines just as harshly.

Some convicts managed to escape into the bush. Before long smallpox and measels and other diseases introduced by the immigrants had drastically reduced the local Aboriginal population. Tribal remnants suddenly started coming into the settlement, although by then the settlers had no need of them. Yet they still wanted the Aborigines' land and water. The settlers seemed to look upon these as something which the Aborigines did not want or did not need. This feeling that the vast resources of Australia are crown land, as if the Aborigines never owned it, is still prevalent.

David McKnight

The demand for Aboriginal artefacts by tourists and museums has made bark painting a profitable activity for some Aborigines. This man borrows the sacred motifs of other tribes and uses them in his own commercial painting.

David McKnight

or by gravitating to the town and living on hand-outs. There was little else that they could do. They had resisted and failed; many soon understood that it was possible to survive only by adapting to a completely different social environment.

In the southern regions of Australia the settlers had no need of the Aborigines. They were regarded more as a pest then anything else. Their land had been taken away from them without payment. Their

(Left) On Bathurst Island, a Roman Catholic priest says prayers for the fishermen. Since the founding of this mission of Northern Australia in 1911, some 850 local Aborigines have become 'Christianized' although most still retain part of their ancient spirit religion.

In 1965, when Queensland gave its Aborigine population the right to vote in state elections, all Australian Aborigines had the franchise. However recent Government legislation to assist the Aborigines and increase their social opportunities has had little effect on their living conditions at grass-roots level in rural conditions.

(Below) Now that more young Aborigines are being given a thorough education, their voice is becoming more assertive in Australian political life. The call is often for the restoration of land to its original tribal owners.

Australian News and Information Bureau

One reason for this widespread disregard for Aboriginal land rights is that the Aborigines were hunters and gatherers. They never tilled the soil, domesticated animals, made cloth, lived in villages or had complex courts of law. The Aborigines were regarded as primitive savages by the majority of the settlers. It seemed to them that the Aborigines wandered about at will picking up their food as they needed it, never putting anything into the soil which would give them a claim of ownership.

The robbing of the Aborigines' land by the settlers effectively undermined their autonomy and whole way of life. The very presence of the settlers affected the supply of game. The Europeans shot wild animals and took over the fresh water supplies for their own stock and for irrigation. Before long they were pushing farms and towns further and further inland and in the face of this intrusion the Aborigines had little choice. They could either stay where they were and die of starvation, or they could retreat and fall back on the tribes behind them and die (for these tribes in turn needed their own land), or they could defend themselves against the Whites' encroachment and die

fighting. They perished in all three ways.

There is a popular belief that the Aborigines were quickly defeated and 'tamed'. But in fact there are many instances where they managed to organize guerilla warfare, in the mountains of New South Wales, in the bush of Cape York Peninsula and in various desert regions. Yet the end of the conflict was a foregone conclusion, because with a hunting and gathering economy it was impossible for the Aborigines to keep an army in the field. This was not the way that the Aborigines were used to organizing their own fights among themselves. To them, fighting was primarily a man to man affair even when both sides were lined up for battle.

Despite the fact that the Aborigines were unable to put an army into the field, that they only had wooden weapons to use against European guns, and they could only travel on foot while the Europeans had horses, nevertheless a stiff resistance was given to the settlers. Gradually, however, one tribe after the other was wiped out or decimated and forced to move off their tribal lands. Some managed to scrape a living by working in peonage for the pastoralists and farmers,

institutions had not been formed there would be a few Aborigines alive today.

Nowadays, the majority of people of Aboriginal descent live on government settlements and missions. Sometimes the Aborigines were coaxed on to these reserves, and sometimes they went of their own free will, for they believed that there was no alternative. But more often than not they were sent there. Various states have different legal definitions as to who is an Aboriginal, so in one state a man might be forced into an institution, while in another he would be free to live in the towns and cities and work where he pleased. It has often been up to the police to decide where an Aborigine should be sent. Families were split up and their members sent to different missions and government settlements. Children of mixed descent were often taken away from their Aboriginal mothers because it was believed that with their 'White blood' they were more intelligent and would more quickly be integrated into the White community. The full-bloods, it was believed, would eventually die out and so the 'Aboriginal problem' would solve itself. Unfortunately half-castes often found themselves in a difficult social situation—never fully accepted either by the Aborigines or by the Europeans.

In the early days the Government settlements and missions were usually run by people who seldom had any special talent or training although undoubtedly the majority of them meant well.

It is unfair to criticize the missionaries and government officials who administer the missions and settlements too much. However, these institutions have overall had a harmful effect. Their aim has been to inculcate European values into the Aborigines and make them reject their own heritage. There has been a systematic attempt to split the generations by taking young children away from their parents and placing them in dormitories. There they have been fed, clothed and educated until old enough to be married or to go to work. In some missions girls were not allowed to leave the dormitories until they were married. The children grew up speaking English while their parents spoke an Aboriginal language, thus creating an unfortunate generation gap.

Until very recently it was seriously believed that Aboriginal children did not have the mental ability to progress beyond the fifth or sixth grade, so few of them received a thorough education. For this reason the number of Aborigines that have studied at university is very small.

Many of the missions and government settlements in the northern regions of Australia are, in effect, reserves of labour. The men leave their wives and children to go out to work as cowboys on large farms. Those who have such jobs can expect to be away for 9 or 10 months, and this

labour was seldom wanted for there was cheap convict and indentured labour. It was believed that the Aborigines would make good citizens and would survive if they received fair and just treatment. For their own good it was decided that the Aborigines should be protected from the evils of civilization, particularly alcohol and the more degenerate settlers. Hence it was decided that there should be special government and mission settlements where the Aborigines could be taught trades, how to farm, read and write and be converted to Christianity. This policy of isolation and protection suited both those who regarded the Aborigines as pests and more trouble than they were worth, and those who believed that given the right conditions they would survive and become useful citizens.

Government settlements and missions for the Aborigines exist to this day and they are a matter of some controversy. On the one hand, the very existence of these institutions gives the impression that nothing positive is being done for the Aborigines. For to isolate people is hardly the way to integrate or assimilate them, it merely maintains them on the periphery of society. On the other hand, if these

David McKnight

These fishermen in the Gulf of Carpentaria show a readiness to adjust to new Western technology. Dinghies and outboard motors have replaced the unstable log rafts they once used. The Aborigines' preference for the old-style hand-made spears, however, remains unchanged.

arrangement has created family problems. The Aborigines are often poorly paid. Indeed it is unusual for them to receive a wage which would support them and their wife and children, and all savings are usually spent during the breaks between work contracts.

Naturally enough, since they have been taught many European values, the Aborigines want many European goods and the only way to get these is by working for money. Unfortunately they have seldom been trained for employment that is well paid. When mining companies move into the reserves where the missions and government settlements are, they often make many promises that the Aborigines will be trained or that the Aborigines will receive a percentage of the profits. But in practice they seldom attempt to train them, they pay them less than Europeans for the same labouring work and company profits rarely reach the local people. It is no wonder that the Aborigines are suspicious of Europeans and regard them as voracious sharks.

Considerable changes in public attitude and government policy towards the Australian Aborigines occurred after the Second World War. Aboriginal matters were given much higher priority and long-standing 'protection' policies were gradu-

ally replaced by more positive legislation. Expenditure on Aboriginal welfare in the Northern Territory by the Federal Government was only $A 126,000 in 1946. A decade later it was nine times that amount and in the 1971-2 financial year the Department of the Interior spent $A 16,330,000 on welfare and advancement programmes.

After an enormous majority in a referendum in 1967, the Australian Constitution was changed to give the Federal Government power to legislate for the Aborigines in all States, and the Aborigines were, for the first time, included in official population census figures. Not long after the referendum, an office for Aboriginal Affairs was established to co-ordinate welfare programmes in the different states. A Minister of Aboriginal Affairs was appointed along with a three-man Council for Aboriginal Affairs to advise the Federal Government on policies.

In early 1972 a five-point 'Statement of Objectives' was drawn up by the Federal Government as a guide for the development of Aboriginal affairs over the next decade. The plan stresses the importance of successful assimilation of the Aborigines into Australian society and strongly opposes a course of separate development. It recognizes the Aborigines' right of self-determination and independence and the need to give special help to many Aborigines in their voluntary transition from a traditional way of life to full participation in Western society.

But in reality, the immediate problems of health, housing, education and vocational training for Aborigines remain a grim indication of the enormous amount to be done before the goals of the Federal Government's plan are achieved.

Unless the Aborigines are given a larger share of Australia's wealth the conflict between the Aborigines and the white Australians will become severe, and the chance for the two races to live in harmony will have been lost. The present problem is nothing like the explosive situation that exists in South Africa or in the US, for the Aboriginal population is still quite small. However, the Aboriginal population is growing faster than the White, and is being supported by radical Melanesian groups in the area e.g. in Vanatua, and Papua New Guinea.

Although by the early 1980s more and more White Australians were showing real concern over the problems of the Aborigines—Federal court judgements have supported land claims such as that to Ayers Rock in 1983—discontent still persists. Constitutionally, Aborigines have been granted full civil rights, but in practice these are often abused—especially where any claims involve valuable mineral resources, and where powerful mining interests are represented. □

The Plumed Serpent

In 1502 when Christopher Columbus discovered the mainland of Central America, he ran up against the land barrier that finally dashed his hopes of finding a westward route to the Indies. Landing at Cape Honduras, he formally claimed the territory for Spain, before following the coastline south. Near the present-day border of Panama and Costa Rica he met people of the country— 'Indians' as they were to him, and so to us, in honour of his immortal mistake.

In the earliest years of exploration the Spanish were drawn to the Caribbean by the urge to colonize and by the spirit of adventure. Vasco Nuñez de Balboa founded a colony in Panama, and won the distinction of being the first European to look on the Pacific. In 1511 Diego Velasquez, meeting little resistance, conquered and occupied Cuba.

Within a few years, a slave-trade had opened up in the Caribbean, as Bay Island Indians were forcibly taken to work in the new Cuban colony. It was with this nascent slave-trade in mind that Velasquez, the first governor of Cuba, offered to support the expedition which left the island in 1517, on condition that the explorers should capture Indians and sell them to him. Bernal Diaz, one of the members of the expedition, wrote in his journal that he and his comrades felt 'it would be against the laws of God and the king for us to turn free men into slaves'. They were motivated, he says, by the simple desire to 'seek new lands in which to try our fortunes and find occupation'. This incident demonstrates two different aspects of the Spanish approach to the process of colonization: on the one hand the unashamed intention to exploit, on the other, the wish to find an outlet for individual energies that would otherwise be thwarted by vested interests.

The expedition of 1517, led by Francisco Hernandez de Cordoba, was a memorable one: for the first time it brought Spaniards into contact with the inhabitants of the Yucatan peninsula of Mexico—the Maya. Before the arrival of the Spanish, Mexico and the rest of Central America had seen the rise and fall of several neolithic

An imaginative reconstruction of Tenochtitlán, the Aztec capital, shows a meeting between Cortez and Montezuma. First received as guests, the Spaniards later had to flee for their lives in the 'night of sorrows'. They later razed Tenochtitlán to the ground and built a new capital, Mexico City.

civilizations, which, based simply on the cultivation of the maize plant, had reached extraordinary heights of sophistication.

By 1517 the culture of the Maya was in decline, having suffered from invasions by other tribes—notably the Toltecs from Central Mexico where the Nahuatl, as opposed to the Maya, language was spoken. The Toltecs were a fiercely militaristic group who probably introduced the Maya to the practice of human sacrifice on a large scale. Cordoba and his followers were impressed by the buildings they saw, but were horrified at the evidence of human sacrifice they encountered, and terrified by the ferocity of the Indians.

Each time the Spaniards landed—once after being cordially invited to do so—they were attacked and driven back to their ships. Eventually they returned to Cuba, but not without some idols and golden ornaments which, appropriately enough, the priest attached to the expedition had filched from a temple while everybody else was engaged in a fierce battle. These objects, of a higher standard of workmanship than anything hitherto found on American soil, caused quite a sensation among the colonists. Some of the more imaginative put down the existence of the idols to the influence of the Jews whom Titus and Vespasian had exiled: ludicrous to modern minds, this conjecture reflects the obsessive concern of the 16th century Spaniard with his own religion. Instead of seeing the idols as manifestations of a totally different religion—as valid in their own way as images of the saints with which they were so familiar—they could only see them as being in direct opposition to Christianity, the work of the Jew, the anti-Christ.

The missionary zeal which the Spanish displayed during and after their conquest of Central America, is sometimes regarded as an ignoble shield for the exploitation of the Indian. Although the Spanish did exploit the Indians, their desire to convert them was genuine enough, and the two issues are really quite separate. In their own eyes, the *Conquistadores*, in bringing Christ to Central America, were simply doing their duty as they conceived it; they were making the Indians the present of eternal life, which otherwise they could never hope to enjoy. The fact that they were simultaneously making their fortunes, and were adding to the extent of the Spanish empire, did not as far as they could see invalidate this service.

Another expedition, launched in the following year at the instigation of Velasquez, fared little better than the first, although its members did manage to obtain a fair amount of gold through barter with the Indians. It also penetrated far enough north along the Mexican coastline for its presence to be noted by

officials of the Aztec empire. At that time the Aztecs held sway over a considerable area of Mexico; the centre of their empire was the magnificent, densely populated island-city of Tenochtitlán on Lake Texcoco in the Valley of Mexico. By 1500 the population of this city numbered a million—a figure that was only equalled by Mexico City, Tenochtitlán's post-Conquest successor, in 1940. To 16th century European eyes it was to seem as impressive as Venice, with its canals, great squares, and stone palaces.

The Aztecs were the latest of the series of tribes who had held hegemony over the peoples of the area. Their regime was highly organized, with a strict hierarchy but yet fairly democratic, at least as far as the Aztecs themselves were concerned. Subjects of the conquered kingdoms found them hard masters, however. An unending stream of tribute paid in kind poured into the city from the outlying territories. Moreover, in order to obtain suitable material for human sacrifice, artificial wars—known as 'flowery wars'—were contrived in which as many prisoners as possible could be captured. The Aztecs worshipped their many gods with great zeal, and most of these required blood to sustain them. Rather like their distant predecessors in the Valley of Mexico, the Toltecs, the Aztecs made a cult of militarism, and supported a warrior élite, divided between the Knights of the Jaguar and the Knights of the Eagle.

The ruling Aztec dynasty claimed descent from the Toltec king, Quetzalcoatl, who had led his followers into Yucatan over 500 years previously. Quetzalcoatl had become a deified cult hero among the Nahua peoples. He had disappeared into the east, but it was believed that he would return from the same direction to claim sovereignty over the Valley of Mexico. No-one believed this legend more devoutly than Montezuma, who was then king of the Aztecs. Myth represented Quetzalcoatl as being bearded and fair-skinned. The year for which he was thought to have forecast his return had been calculated to be 1519—the very same year, tragically enough for Montezuma's peace of mind, in which Hernando Cortez landed on the coast where later the city of Vera Cruz was founded.

In August 1521, less than three years after he had set out from Cuba, Cortez had brought about the downfall of the Aztec Empire. The story of Cortez's conquest of Mexico—or 'New Spain', as it was called throughout the Spanish colonial period—is a remarkable one. Cortez set out with 508 soldiers, 100 seamen (who were later drawn into active military service as casualties took their toll of the soldiers), 16 horses and 14 cannon. Although they later received reinforcements from Cuba, the Spaniards

Thomas Hoepker/John Hillelson Agency

Indian labour formed the basis of the Spanish colonial empire. Under the encomienda system many Indians became the virtual slaves of their Spanish masters, even though this was against the wishes of the government in Spain.

were at all times heavily outnumbered.

Certain things were on their side: the Indians had never seen horses before, and at first they took horse and rider to be the same animal. Cannon were a new phenomenon also, and created much confusion. Too much, however, can be made of these points. The Indians soon became accustomed to the horses and the cannon, and ceased to see them as alarming evidences of supernatural power. More worrying to the Aztec leadership was the apparent correspondence between

the Quetzalcoatl legend and the appearance of fair-skinned, bearded men from the east.

Montezuma's uncertainty as to how to deal with the Spaniards was to be his undoing. If he had attacked them early on with the full force of his armies, there is no doubt that Cortez would have had to withdraw. As it was, Cortez had time during his march to Tenochtitlán to win over a considerable amount of local support, both from among the discontented subjects of the Empire and from the Indians of Tlaxcala, an independent republic which laboured under the continual threat of Aztec aggression. That Cortez was able to enlist in his favour the enemies of the Aztecs was undoubtedly the biggest single reason for his victory.

During the next decade, Honduras, Guatemala, El Salvador and Nicaragua were brought under the Spanish umbrella, as the *Conquistadores* sought new areas to subjugate. Nicaragua formed an exception in being colonized by the Spaniards of Panama. Costa Rica, at first inimical to settlement, was the last to be colonized. The Mexican colony flourished, attracting many settlers. Mexico City replaced Tenochtitlán as the capital. Built on the ruins of the former city, within a hundred years it had substituted a Baroque magnificence of its own for the massive geometrical grandeur of its predecessor. The work of Indian craftsmen gave a distinctively Mexican look to the designs of colonial architects.

The Spaniards imported many animals hitherto unknown in Mexico—cattle, sheep, pigs and goats. They also introduced European crops, vegetables and fruit trees which flourished alongside the immemorial plantations of maize and maguey, the cactus from which the Indians derived their liquor. In Mexico the 17th century saw the birth of a cultural movement which produced poets, playwrights and architects of a very high standard, together with historians of the Conquest and of the pre-Columbian past.

The basis of the material property which made all this possible was the labour of the Indian. In a sense there was some element of continuity: instead of paying taxes and performing labour services for the Aztecs, the Indians of Mexico—Aztecs included—did the same for the Spanish. Similarly, in the other Central American colonies, the Indians were taken advantage of.

In the early years, Indian services and tribute were exacted through the means

Cornell Capa/Magnum

of the *encomienda* system, a species of feudalism already entrenched in Spain's West Indian possessions. The system consisted of the allocation of groups of Indians to favoured colonists, who, in return for instructing them in the Christian religion and supplying them with housing, clothing and so on, were entitled to demand tribute and labour services.

Although in theory the *encomienda* could be seen as a benevolent arrangement designed to benefit the Indian, in practice it usually turned out quite differently. The system had been much abused in the West Indies, where it had led to depopulation and had been hardly distinguishable from slavery. Cortez introduced it into Mexico very much against the will of Charles V, who at the time of the Conquest was thinking of doing away with it altogether. He had been much affected by the anti-*encomienda* propaganda of Bartolome de Las Casas, the Dominican friar later to be known as the 'Protector of the Indians' in recognition of his solicitude for their welfare. However, when the royal order forbidding the issue of *encomiendas* reached Mexico in 1523, they were already an established fact.

It soon became apparent that in all the Central American colonies, as elsewhere in the Spanish Empire, the system invited abuse. *Encomenderos* showed themselves to be incapable of keeping their side of the bargain, and exploited the Indians mercilessly. By 1550, however, the *en-*

comienda was in decline partly as a result of the 'New Laws' of 1542, which reflected the growing influence of Las Casas and others like him, in their prohibition of any further *encomiendas,* and which decreed that the Indian was to be treated as a vassal of the Spanish king.

As the *ecomienda* disappeared, the Indian came more directly under the control of the vice-regal government. Each Indian community came under the jurisdiction of the *corregidor,* or magistrate, who was responsible for the welfare of

(Above) Many Central Americans are poor and homeless. These migrant labourers are camping under arc lights in the main square of Santa Anna, in El Salvador.

(Below) Not all the indigenous peoples of Central America came under Spanish colonial rule. These Indians from Panama are said to speak a form of Elizabethan English and to be partly descended from British buccaneers.

Popperfoto

the Indian as well as for the collection of taxes and the dispensation of justice. Labour services were rationed according to a rotational system known as the *repartimiento*, which in theory ensured that the Indians were not worked into the ground.

However well-intentioned the provisions of the Spanish government, they were always liable to abuse by the colonists. As a rule, the descendants of the original settlers who had been born in the colony, the Creoles, tended to treat the Indians worse than the central government or its representatives in Mexico. Spaniards born in Spain, known as *gachupines*, were regarded with distrust by the Creoles, and rivalry between the two factions played a large part in colonial affairs.

Not all Indians were reduced to the same level, however; the descendants of the Aztec aristocracy were accorded some measure of prestige, and were entitled to call themselves 'Don'. In the countryside the children of pre-Columbian chieftains sometimes made the transition into the colonial age as *encomenderos* in their own right. Below them in the social scale, and rapidly growing in number came the *mestizos*, or people of mixed race, who formed a kind of lower middle class. The Indian of the country districts lived a life not very different from that lived before the Conquest. Worse off were the Indians of Mexico City, who had been edged out onto the outskirts of the town, where they lived in miserable hovels, and were usually forced to find work as unskilled labourers. Even skilled workmen among them found it virtually impossible to enter a craft guild. Unluckiest of all were the 'wild' Indians who had been captured in frontier districts, or those already working as slaves in the Indian communities, for these were allowed to be used as slaves in the mines.

As a rule though, Indians could not legally be used as slaves, with the result that a new element was soon introduced into the population—the Negro. In 1524 Gil Gonzalez de Avila had brought some Africans with him to Honduras. In the next century it is probable that more Negroes came to the isthmus than Europeans. Coming as a rule to Honduras, they gradually became distributed throughout Central America. In later times more Negroes arrived on the Caribbean coast as free labourers—in the 19th century to work on the banana plantations, and in the 20th to help build the Panama Canal.

In Mexico City in 1625, according to Thomas Gage, an English Dominican friar, there were 50,000 Negroes and mulattoes, both slaves and freedmen; and only 80,000 Indians and *mestizos*. By the 17th century the Indian population of the Valley of Mexico had

fallen alarmingly. From a figure of well over a million in 1519 it had dropped to about 70,000. From this low point the population rose to 275,000 by the end of the colonial period. Although the changes effected by the Spanish in the environmental setting may have had something to do with it, the chief cause for this spectacular decline was disease—various infections which had entered New Spain with the Spaniard and against which the Indian had no resistance.

As in Mexico, the Indian population of Central America was much reduced by disease. In the early years of the colonial period, the Spanish mixed freely with the few survivors, forming the basis of the predominantly *mestizo* population. In Guatemala, where the Indians were less affected by epidemics, and where there was a larger Indian population to start with, there is today a high proportion—

The economic power of the United States causes much local resentment and hostility in Central America. Salvadorian students demonstrate against American aid, which they believe is used as an instrument of imperialism.

over half—of pure-bred Indians. In Costa Rica the Indian population was drastically reduced, and so today this country has the largest community of people of unmixed European descent.

In Mexico the depopulation of the 17th century tended to the advantage of a new land-owning class: the *hacendados*, replacing the *encomenderos* and enjoying much more freedom of action. As land became vacant, private owners acquired it with ease, building up enormous estates, or *haciendas*, which functioned as self-contained communities, largely immune from outside interference. The Indians who were obliged to work for these concerns, bereft of their access to communal land, were kept in a state of virtual serfdom. The *hacienda* survived as an institution into the years of Mexican independence, and at the time of the Revolution in 1910, two-thirds of the land was held by 836 proprietors. Not until the Presidency of Lazaro Cardenas (1934–40) were the big estates broken up into communal lands.

In colonial times, the only factor which came between the Indian and the ruthlessness of the colonist—apart from the rather ineffectual paternalistic efforts of

Cornell Capa/Magnum

religions, in all their subtlety, had been lost with the destruction of these cultures: very little of these religions remained. Human sacrifice was still practised secretly in the 17th century, but with none of the ceremony that might have sanctified it originally. In some cases victims were given the name of Jesus Christ and crucified, perhaps in order to neutralize the power of Christianity, or maybe to turn it to fresh account. Such actions testify to the confusion and resentment that must have sometimes existed in the Indian mind.

Still, the Catholic religion gave to the Indians of Central America something which the North American Indian never received at the hand of the Anglo-Saxon settlers: a place in the cosmos and in the society of the conquering people. Even though the Indians were admitted at the very bottom of society, they were admitted. Although their old gods had apparently deserted him, they were given a new spiritual framework in which to place their existence, a justification for life and death. The fact that old beliefs were incorporated in the new, gave the resulting synthesis vigour.

By no means all the Central American Indians were exposed to Spanish culture during the colonial period. For example, some tribes of northern Mexico, and the Lacandón of Chiapas were undefeated when the Spanish Empire ended—occupying as they did territories which had little to attract the colonist, and which gave them plenty of room for manoeuvre. These people had survived to the present day with their individuality very largely intact.

The most obvious exception in Central America is British Honduras, or Belize as it became in 1973. This was the only officially non-Hispanic territory—although much of the sparsely settled Caribbean coastal region from Belize to Panama, has had very little Spanish

(Above) Units of the Mexican Navy parade on Independence Day. Since Mexico and the Central American republics gained independence in 1821 they have built up a strong national identity.

(Below) Although the Tarahumara have adopted Catholicism, many of their old customs survive. On Good Friday they gather for a ceremony which combines both Christian and Tarahumara beliefs.

the central government—was the concern shown by the Catholic Church, as exemplified by the work of the various orders of friars which had arrived in the wake of the *Conquistadores*. In general, the friars were motivated by an altruistic zeal for the welfare of the Indian, who, once inside the Church, was the equal of any man. The success of Spanish missionary endeavours was at the same time partial and complete: while Roman Catholicism became the nominal religion of those Indians who were brought into contact with the Church, their pre-Conquest spiritual beliefs and traditions lingered on beneath its veneer. Their religion was syncretic, that is, a combination of Christian and pagan beliefs.

To begin with, the continuation of pre-Conquest practices was a gesture of cultural independence and survival. The higher mysteries of the Aztec and Mayan

Burt Glinn/Magnum

(Above) The introduction of horses and cattle by the Spanish allowed the development of cattle ranching. Horses are still widely used, and Mexican cowboys take a fierce pride in their riding skill.

influence. The first settlers were Englishmen from Jamaica, who came around 1640 and brought their slaves with them. Reluctantly tolerated by the Spanish, the British were well established in the region by 1821, when the Central American states became independent.

Belize has more in common with the British West Indies than with Central America, in that more than half the population are English-speaking mulattoes or Negroes, while the indigenous Mayan Indians only make up 17 per cent. About 10 per cent is composed of Black Caribs: descendants of freed or escaped slaves who absorbed the culture of the Island Caribs. Of the remainder, 10 per cent are of unmixed European descent, most of them German-speaking Mennonites who originally fled from Russia in search of religious freedom, although the number of North American residents is increasing. Belize has served as a place of refuge for political and other refugees from the neighbouring countries, while among its racially varied population there are also some Arabs and Chinese. Representatives of these races are to be found elsewhere in Central America, having come of their own volition to engage in trade, with the exception of some coolies imported into the isthmus of Tehuantepec in Mexico to work on the transcontinental railway.

Similarly non-Hispanic in character is the eastern coastline of Nicaragua, the 'Mosquito Coast', where the Miskito have come into contact with the British and later with North Americans, rather than with the Spanish; only in 1860 did Britain recognize Nicaragua's sovereignty over this territory. Protestant missions predominate over Catholic ones, and the English language is more commonly spoken than Spanish, the official language of the country. Before a regular airline service began from Managua, the Mosquito Coast was more easily accessible from New Orleans than from the Nicaraguan capital.

The Miskito incorporate a large Negroid element in their racial make-up: a slave ship wrecked off the coast around 1640 is thought to have laid the basis of this mixture, which was strengthened by the addition of fugitive slaves from the West Indies and the Honduran mines. The name 'Miskito' itself derives, not from mosquito, but either from the phrase '*Indios mixtos*', or alternatively from the muskets with which British buccaneers supplied them in the 17th century. Between the pirates and the Miskito there existed a kind of alliance of convenience, and Miskito Indians sometimes accompanied them on their excursions. The culture of the Miskito today can only be interpreted in the light of their 300 year relationship with the White man: they hardly existed as such before this contact, and it is likely that their acculturation was voluntary in the first place.

Returning to the Hispanic territories of Central America today, one finds that the *mestizo*, or *ladino*, predominates. As the Spaniards hastened to impose their religion on the Indians, so they lost no time in starting to absorb them racially through miscegenation. In Mexico, five per cent only of the people claim pure European descent, 25 per cent are Indians, and the remainder are *mestizos*, some of whom have Negro blood in addition. As in the other Central American countries, practically everyone speaks Spanish, although many of the Indians are bi-lingual, their aboriginal language being their native tongue. In Guatemala, about half the people are pure-blooded Indians, while the rest are mainly *mestizos*. In El Salvador, the most densely populated Central American country, *mestizos* make up 75 per cent of the population; Honduras has an even higher *mestizo* proportion of 90 per cent and also incorporates a large Black element along the northern coast. In Nicaragua and Panama, *mestizos* predominate. Costa Rica, the smallest of the republics, is an exception in that most of its inhabitants are of purely European stock.

Radical discrimination as such can hardly be said to exist in Mexico and Central America: it is a totally foreign concept. The class structure is only vaguely related to colour—although the

'Indian' is still at the bottom of the social ladder, the *mestizo* or *ladino* in the middle, and the European, comparatively rare as he is, at the top. These are no longer racial terms, however, but cultural ones. The Indian can become a *ladino* by deserting the Indian dress and language, and adopting a European life-style along with the Spanish tongue. Many *ladinos* are pure-bred Indians, while many who are Indian in their culture are *mestizos* by birth. When a *ladino* owes nothing at all culturally to the Indian element in his descent, he considers himself, and is considered by others, to be as good as any Spaniard.

How this social mobility operates in practice can be seen by looking at the town of Ticul, in Western Yucatan. Following the decline of the henequen plantations during the 1940s, the local shoe and hat-making industries became large employers of skilled labour. Although half of the population of the district still live in the Indian manner and cultivate their own plots of land, the word 'Indian', with its connotations of backwardness, is hardly ever used except as a term of abuse; '*mestizo*' is used to cover both the pure-blood Indian and the part-bred Indian who live in the old fashion. Here, the '*catrines*' are the hispanicized members of society. Indians who leave the land to work in either of the craft industries have a better chance of doing well if they speak Spanish and adopt European dress—if they become, in fact, *catrines*. Once a small financial outlay is made to obtain the trappings of White people, the self-made *catrine,* however much an Indian by descent, is no longer barred by any social prejudice from achieving a higher standard of living. Money combined with the will to conform to a European ideal is the key to material success.

Peasant farming is looked down on as an Indian way of life which also yields very little in the way of profit. In traditional Indian communities, any profit made by the farmer does not become financial capital, but is used to sponsor religious ceremonies. The spending of money in this way, rather than its mere possession, is the means of gaining prestige in the Indian community. An interesting result of this is that in some cases Indians in fairly remote villages have been known to embrace Protestantism, partly in order to escape from the financial obligation inseparable from being a member of the local Catholic community. Participation in the *cofradias*, or religious brotherhoods, which represent folk Catholicism, involves fairly high expenditure. Similarly, drinking is an integral part of religious festivals. This, apart from being expensive in itself, leads to alcoholism and a consequent loss of working time. Conversion to Protestant-

Although North American companies have largely replaced the Spanish aristocracy as landowners, Central America is still dominated by Plantation economics. At a Standard Fruit Company Packing Station, bananas are washed for export.

ism can thus be seen as one way out of the traditional pattern of communal poverty.

Social equality in Central America is still an ideal rather than a reality. In Guatemala, despite attempts at land reform, 70 per cent of the land is owned by two per cent of all landowners. In Mexico, the Indians—both ethnically and culturally speaking—who form a third of the total population, live below the subsistence level, while half of all Mexicans live in conditions of desperate poverty. Fifty-one per cent of the national income is pocketed by one per cent of the population. With these figures before one it is evident that the Revolution has

failed. Despite a certain pride in Mexican nationality, the dominant element in modern Mexico is the nearness of the United States. As a result the destructive capitalist values of a consumer society have gained considerable acceptance. Many Mexicans visit the States each year in search of seasonal employment.

In Guatemala, Honduras and to a lesser extent in Nicaragua vast territories are owned by the United Fruit Company and by the Standard Fruit Company, (both North American concerns). The possession of such economic interests has led to repeated interference by the United States in Central American politics. In 1954, for example, Jacopo Arbenz Guzman, the left-wing president of Guatemala, was forced to resign because his agrarian reforms threatened the United Fruit Company's holding in Central America, and North American economic imperialism replaced Spanish colonialism. Guerrilla warfare continues in the area into the 1980s.

Cornell Capa/Magnum

The Trail of Tears

Ernst Haas/Magnum

At the end of the 15th century the feudal system of Europe was crumbling and a number of clearly-defined, competitive nation-states were emerging from its ruins. The continent's concerted effort against Islam was giving way to fanatical religious factionalism within Christendom itself, and trade and exploration created a fierce rivalry for the discovery and exploitation of new commercial markets. The idea that the world might be spherical rather than flat even prompted voyagers to seek the wealth of the Orient by sailing west rather than heading round Africa's southern coast.

The 'discovery' of America by Columbus in 1492 resulted almost inevitably in violent competition between the European powers for the New World and its resources. Despite the fact that they professed widely-differing motives, however, and frequently warred among themselves, the White people who colonized America during the next three centuries shared a common cultural heritage and a number

A cinema reconstruction of a Crow encampment captures the idyllic aspect of the Indian legend. The horse, introduced by White People, and the skin tipi gave the Plains Tribes great mobility—but their age of glory lasted only 100 years.

of assumptions that profoundly affected their relations with the native population.

They all came from large, autocratic societies that measured prestige in terms of private property and a rigid class system; they all believed ardently in different versions of the same intolerant religion; they were all dedicated to the accumulation of wealth and power, either in the name of an absolute sovereign or—especially in Protestant northern Europe—by and for the enterprizing individual; and they all demonstrated a growing faith in the superiority and infallibility of their own civilization. With all the limitations and impatience of this background, they came upon the

inhabitants of a world that had been in virtual isolation for at least 10,000 years.

The 650 or so native societies, with a total population of perhaps 3,500,000, which occupied the area north of Mexico at the time of Columbus, were far more diverse than the Europeans who 'discovered' them. They ranged from tiny hunting bands of one or two families in the far north to prosperous farming towns, with complex social and religious structures and advanced artistic skills, in the southeast. Their various habitats included arctic tundra, sub-arctic forest, mountain valleys, lush temperate zones, open grasslands and sub-tropical desert. Yet the majority of Indian societies had certain important characteristics in common.

To begin with, while European technology had been concerned largely with the development of means of transport and warfare, the Indians had concentrated on evolving closer and more efficient adjustments to their own natural environ-

Western Americana Picture Library

French fur trappers moved into Canaaa early in the 16th century, building up a thriving business. Indians soon became part of a trading network which crossed the continent, hunting in small bands.

ments. The very variety of their ways of life was the result of the same fundamental approach being applied to a multiplicity of different regions and climates.

The Eskimo hunting band, feeding, clothing and housing itself in the perilous and forbidding conditions of the arctic, showed the same underlying attitudes to the world as the Pueblo farming community of the southwest, which provided food and sustained a rich culture by cultivating a desert many White people regarded as a barren wasteland. The native Americans' technological genius lay in their ability to recognize and exploit the full potential of everything that grew or lived in their area without upsetting the basic balance between flora, fauna and humans.

Another common feature of Indian societies north of the Rio Grande was their comparatively small size. At the time of Columbus some of the rich agricultural towns of the southeast were forming into political confederacies of many thousands of people like their great Mexican neighbours before them, but

most of the other North American Indians probably spent the greater part of their lives in social units little larger than a village, coming together with other bands only for warfare or to celebrate annual festivals.

The size of these groups prevented the emergence of institutions that could enforce conformity on those who would not co-operate willingly. Everyone was required in the day-to-day business of living—the men to hunt or fish, farm or gather wild plants, or fight; the women to bear children, prepare food, tend the home and perhaps cultivate fields. There simply were not enough resources for a ruling élite, a standing army, a police system or any of the other organizations which governed and kept order in Europe.

The Indians' solution to this problem —how to conduct the relationship between a person and his society, each of which needed, but could not compel, the other—was to emphasize the need for harmony at every level of life. Children were taught by story, precept and example that they should be courageous, uncomplaining, unassertive and uncompetitive, and that the pursuit of personal power or wealth was ignoble and contemptible.

A leader—often an outstanding warrior or hunter—was usually acknowledged, but he could only poersuade, not enjoin.

In 1838 President Andrew Jackson ignored a Supreme Court order protecting Cherokee lands in the Southeast. 4,000 Cherokees died on a forced march to Oklahoma: the Trail of Tears.

A decision affecting the whole group had to be unanimous. Dissenters were not bound by it, and if they seriously disagreed they might leave the band and try to join another. A person was trained and expected to consider community before self, but the ultimate arbiter of what was right was his or her own conscience. No-one else had authority over that.

The concern with harmonious relationships between individual and group and between group and environment, which typified many native societies, also lay at the root of the religious systems that underpinned their vision of life. The things which made life possible—sun, air, water, earth and spiritual forces— were common to all people and were sacred. They therefore could not be owned; the produce of a particular area might be assigned to a family or a group, but it would have been both sacrilegious and absurd to suggest that the soil itself belonged to anyone.

Many Indians thus found the concept of land as private property incomprehensible and repugnant; and this, com-

Western Americana Picture Library

Western Americana Picture Library

bined with differences between native and European notions of government, created much of the disastrous misunderstanding between North American Indian and White people.

The first meeting between these two worlds, following Columbus' discovery, came in 1501 when the Portuguese explorer Gaspar Cortoreal landed on a bleak stretch of coast and, having been hospitably received by the local hunting Indians, kidnapped 57 of them to take home as slaves. On the return journey Cortoreal's boat sank, and only seven Indians reached Europe alive, but the place from which they had come was named 'Labrador' to signify that it was an abundant source of labour material.

The next major contacts came at the opposite end of the region, with a series of Spanish expeditions, pushing up from Mexico and Central America in the search of gold and new lands. Hernando de Soto, a veteran of the conquest of Peru, determined 'to make the Indians stand in terror of the Spaniards' as he travelled through the country of the prosperous southeastern farmers, and he left a trail of bloodshed, kidnapping and the wholesale burning of villages before he died in 1542 and his men withdrew in disarray.

For a while the Spaniards confined their activities north of Mexico to a

missionary effort in Florida, but in 1598 Juan de Onate led a large force into the southwest to extend the military and economic empire of the Spanish crown and ensure the salvation of the Indians' souls. The peaceful Pueblos along the Rio Grande were soon conquered, their religious societies and seasonal ceremonies were suppressed, and they were bound by the *encomienda* system to serve and support the priests who had come to convert them, as well as the soldiers sent to keep them in order and protect them from Apache and other roaming Indian raiders from the plains. By 1610, when a capital was founded at Santa Fé, New Spain's northern frontier province seemed secure.

In the northeast, meanwhile, relationships of a different kind had been forming between White people and Indians. During the 16th century French and English fishermen working off the coast of Newfoundland had bartered for furs with Algonkin, Naskapi and other migratory hunting peoples, and with the more settled Hurons along the St Lawrence River. The fur traders, particularly the French were more successful than most White groups in their relations with the natives. This was partly because they had no interest in saving Indian souls or taking Indian land; indeed they valued, often shared, the way of life of the peoples who

Spain invaded California in 1769, and many Indian communities were converted by Jesuit missionaries. A second 'invasion' 70 years later decimated the peaceful population —the brutal Gold Rush.

provided their livelihood, frequently taking Indian wives, speaking Indian languages and raising their children in an Indian culture.

The Indians, for their part, initially benefited greatly from the exchange. The iron axes, chisels and other European tools for which they traded were far more efficient than the laboriously-made native equivalents of bone, stone and wood, and firearms soon showed their superiority over bows and arrows, clubs and spears. The greater efficiency of the White people's technology more than compensated for the fact that the Indians, obliged to trap for furs, had less time to devote to hunting for food, and for a while many bands enjoyed unprecedented prosperity.

But a tribe which used European goods quickly lost the skills and habits that had enabled it to be self-sufficient; when over-killing left successive regions without adequate stocks of fur-bearing animals, the peoples living there were deprived of the means to survive by either the old methods or the new. This accentuated tribal conflicts over land and drove the traders, and reliance on White goods, deeper and deeper into the continent leaving in their wake peoples who had lost much of their resilience and independence by the time the next wave of White people appeared.

For the moment, however, more prolonged White contact was still confined to a small but growing part of the south and east. During the first quarter of the 17th century, while the Spanish were consolidating their hold on Florida, the first English colony was founded as a commercial enterprise by a group of adventurers at Jamestown, Virginia, further north along the Atlantic Coast, and the Dutch started a trading settlement in what is now New York.

In the same period, a number of English Puritan groups, seeking the freedom to practise their own religions and ways of life, colonized parts of the area north and east of the Dutch, and further north still the French settled Port Royal in modern Nova Scotia and started to extend west along the St Lawrence. Nearly all the coastal regions into which White settlers were now moving were densely populated by rich communities of settled farming Indians, some of them organized into fairly sizeable confederacies and with —for Indians—rigid class systems.

These nations extended an almost uniform, if cautious, welcome to the newcomers, taught them how to live in the strange North American land, traded with them and sold them plots of territory for their fields, villages and plantations. For a while, as in fur-trading areas, the contact seemed to be mutually beneficial; then, usually as a result of the Whites' apparently insatiable appetite for land and contemptuous disregard for local custom, relations degenerated and finally broke down completely into vicious and brutal warfare.

The first major conflict came in 1622, when chiefship of the Powhatan Confederacy on part of whose land the Jamestown settlement had been founded, passed to Opechancanough, an elderly man who feared that the English aimed to dispossess his entire people. He attacked the colony, but was repulsed; when he tried again in 1644, aged over 90, his worst fears were justified; the colonists were strong enough to smash the confederacy, burn the fields and sack the villages. Opechancanough, already exhausted and dying, was captured and then needlessly shot.

Other wars in the new colonies followed a similar pattern. The most serious and famous of them, King Philip's War, which ended in 1696 after years of brutal fighting on both sides, saw the destruction of the southern New England tribes by fervent Puritans who believed the Indians to be agents of Satan and exulted, during the final firing of the Pequot stronghold, that 'God is over us. He laughs His

TECUMTHA.

Tecumseh, a Shawnee prophet and military leader, made the only real attempt to unite the Indians against the Whites. But tribal rivalries undermined the movement and it collapsed in 1812.

By the 19th century, many Plains Tribes were dependent on the bison for their food and clothing. In 1870, Congress authorized a new campaign—and 60 million bison were slaughtered in 40 years.

enemies to scorn, making them as a fiery oven'.

There were many reasons why the Indians were always defeated eventually in the colonial wars. Probably the single most important factor, however, was the disastrous effect of European diseases. The Indians had no resistance against smallpox, TB or measles, among others. They were so weakened by these illnesses, particularly in populous settlements where the infection spread easily, that they were—as a modern Indian leader

has pointed out—roughly in the situation that would have confronted medieval Europe if a massive onslaught of militarily-sophisticated invaders had taken place after the worst ravages of the Black Death. The combined catastrophes of epidemic, warfare and cultural clash demoralized and bewildered the Indians and prevented them from driving out the colonists in the vital period when a victory for the natives was still possible.

Settlers, meanwhile, were continuing to stream in from Europe. The largest numbers were religious dissenters and fortune-seekers from England. In 1682 William Penn signed a treaty with the Delaware Indians south of New York— which had been newly-won from the Dutch—by which he received land for the Quaker commonwealth and commercial venture of Pennsylvania. Despite the growing intrusions, however, there was relatively little serious warfare between natives and settlers for the next 80 years or so. Penn's Quakers were among the few White groups to honour their treaty commitments scrupulously, and relations with the local Indians remained cordial.

Elsewhere in America the intensifying rivalry between European powers—particularly France and Britain—for possession of the continent gave the Indians a military significance and made the White authorities anxious not to offend them lest they joined the opposing side.

A major stabilizing factor in this situation was the position of the Iroquois League of Five Nations, which occupied much of the present-day New York State and held sway over a far greater area. At the end of the 17th century the Iroquois, impoverished by the decline of the fur trade in their region, completely destroyed the neighbouring French-backed Huron Confederacy for control of the trade with interior Canada, and since then they had been extending their authority over more and more of the northeast.

The remnants of defeated tribes were adopted into the Iroquois and numbers were further swelled by the arrival of other peoples who had been displaced by Whites, like the Tuscaroras, who in the middle of the 18th century moved up from the southern colonies to form the sixth nation of the League. Dependent tribes were given protection, forbidden to negotiate with Europeans except through the League leadership, and moved into areas that had been depopulated through disease to prevent vacuums of territory, to which the colonists might feel they had a justified claim.

The Iroquois' constitution, their diplomatic skill and military might, made them the most feared and respected of the Indians and in 1763, when they emerged from the Seven Years' War victorious with their English allies, their position was even stronger. In the same year a serious uprising by Pontiac, an Ottowa chief, and a number of tribes that had sided with the French and feared English encroachments on their lands, prompted George III to issue a Proclamation defining the colonies' boundaries, setting aside all territory west of the Appalachians as Indian country, and providing that all purchases of land must in future be made only through the Crown in order to avoid exploitation and misunderstanding.

The colonists were sceptical about the plan; George Washington, for instance, staked out a plot for himself beyond the Proclamation limits, confident that the document was merely 'a temporary expedient to quiet the minds of the Indians'. When the Government made some efforts to implement the proposals, instructing governors to remove and charge intruders on native territory, the colonists, especially frontiersmen like Daniel Boone, who was a surveyor employed by land speculators, grew angry and frustrated. Their annoyance was one factor in the outbreak of hostilities between the colonies and Crown in 1776.

In the 280 or so years between the 'discovery' of America and the close of the War of Independence considerably less than one-fifth of the present United States and Canada had been occupied by Europeans. The next century was to see the conquest of the vast remaining area. In 1769 the Spaniards had invaded California and gained control over the peaceful food-gathering and fishing peoples of the coast. With the power of the Iroquois—four of whose Six Nations had sided with the British Crown—finally broken in the United States, and with an end to hostilities between the Europeans, the White Americans were free to turn their attention to the consolidation of their empires.

In the Northwest Ordinance of 1787, the United States established rules for dealing with Indians that were essentially a continuation of the legalistic, cautious British policy, but they could not be enforced; it was impossible to police the entire frontier, and settlers and prospectors were daily trespassing on Indian land in defiance of the law and thus creating friction with the natives.

Official attitudes and assumptions, moreover, were changing. The 18th century administrators—worldly, tolerant aristocrats in London who viewed the 'Noble Savage' with a mixture of amusement and admiration, and earnest Virginian gentlemen with classical educations and principles—were replaced increasingly during the 19th century by policy-makers with different aims and backgrounds.

Frontiersmen like President Andrew Jackson often had a deep and powerful hatred for the Indians, and the ideals of Victorian America were profoundly unsympathetic to traditional native cultures. The rise of evangelical Christianity, extolling industry, sobriety and the sanctity of the individual, and the admission of millions of immigrants who

The massacre of 300 defenceless Sioux at Wounded Knee in 1890 was the ugly finale of military action against the Indians. The frozen corpse of Chief Big Foot was photographed lying in the snow.

Henri Cartier-Bresson/Magnum

were to be given a new chance, free from the shackles of outmoded European societies, bred a vision of America as a land of unlimited opportunity, a signpost to the future of the world.

Later in the century, Darwin's *Theory of Evolution* lent weight to the notion that the progress of White civilization was a 'Manifest Destiny', to which the remaining native nations were a temporary obstacle; and in this atmosphere it was easy to see the Indians as a doomed race, whose final disappearance was both inevitable and right. If any individuals should by chance survive, they were to be delivered over to philanthropists to have their indolent, childlike natures trained to the virtues of Protestant America.

In the first decade of the 19th century Tecumseh, a Shawnee prophet and military leader of extraordinary vision and great skill, recognized what was happening and made the first, and last, serious attempt to turn the tide that was running against native North America. He saw that despite local treaties and alliances between the Whites and individual peoples, the advancing frontier was a catastrophe that would ultimately destroy all the Indians unless they could unite against it.

Tecumseh travelled ceaselessly among the free tribes and nations, trying to rally them in a united stand along a line from the Great Lakes to the Gulf of Mexico; but although he achieved some measure of support from groups of Potawatomis, Ojibwas, Winnebagos and others, his effort came too late in history, when the White population of the continent had already long overtaken the Indian. Tribal enmities, corrupted leaders and the traditional lack of a means to compel dissenters in Indian societies, all led to splits and defections and when the British abandoned their native allies at the end of the War of 1812 the Indians' solidarity

Apathy and alcoholism are the modern enemies of the American Indian. The loss of purpose has left only abhorrence of the White society for which Indians are chronically ill-equipped.

Indians today are the poorest ethnic minority in America. New organizations like the militant AIM demand justice—the improvement of Indian conditions without the loss of identity.

Michelle Vignes/John Hillelson Agency

collapsed. With it died Tecumseh's vision of an autonomous, permanent Indian nation, and the last hope that White and native America might live together in peace and with mutual independence and respect.

With pressure on land continuously increasing, the Government decided to settle all the eastern Indians west of the Mississippi, where they would be able to live 'in perpetuity'. There were a number of small wars and skirmishes, but the Indians were hopelessly outnumbered and in 1832 the defeat of the Sac and Fox chief, Black Hawk, virtually ended the struggle for the Great Lakes and the eastern Plains.

In Georgia, Alabama, Florida and some of the other states of the southeast, however, the battle went on longer. There, the so-called 'Five Civilized Tribes', who were descended from pre-Columbian farming confederacies and had integrated their cultures successfully and prosperously with the White civilization that had grown up about them, were ordered to leave despite the fact that they were Christianized, law-abiding, peaceful, had inter-married with the White community and had signed treaties with the Government for what remained to them of the land their ancestors had occupied.

With great hardship the Choctaws, Chickasaws and Creeks were moved, but the Cherokees fought in the courts, ultimately taking their case to the Supreme Court, where it was upheld by Chief Justice John Marshall. President Andrew Jackson promptly replied: 'The Chief Justice has rendered his decision; now let him enforce it'. Marshall was powerless to do so, and in 1838 and 1839 the army

Reservation life is not uniformly depressed—the Navajos have exploited their lands in Arizona with great enterprise. But even here the individual Indian remains poor.

was sent to evict the Indians. On the journey from their fertile homelands to the hot and disease-ridden Oklahoma area, 4,000 of the 14,000 Cherokees who had set out lost their lives, and the trek became known as 'The Trail of Tears'.

The pattern for the conquest of the rest of America was much the same: White intrusion on tribal territory sparked off wars that the Indians inevitably lost; treaties guaranteeing reservations or land further west were signed, only to be broken a few years later by further encroachments that resulted in renewed violence and new peace agreements even less advantageous to the Indians.

The situation was worsened by the fact that White and Indian signatories were not really able to enforce their respective sides of the bargains; young braves, anxious to prove their courage, often provoked and harried Whites in defiance of the views of the tribal elders, while American traders and prospectors frequently contravened treaties by crossing or seizing Indian land.

The Canadian Government, anxious to avoid the bitterness and violence that had occurred south of the border, allowed no settlers into the west until the nomadic hunting tribes had ceded their land to the Crown and been confined, band by band, to tiny, isolated widely-scattered reserves. The effect, however, was the same: to deprive the Indians of the land base and mobility on which their cultures and economies were founded.

The Gold Rush in California in the 1840s and 1850s, and the growing settlements in Texas, New Mexico and other parts of the southwest, were the immediate causes of the last series of major Indian wars. Those Californian natives who had not been settled and Christianized by the Spaniards lived mainly in the interior valleys, following a peaceful, primitive food-gathering existence. The effect of an invasion by gold-prospectors was to

deplete the population disastrously, largely through disease but partly also through violence, and bewildered Indians had neither the numbers nor the inclination to resist effectively.

In the Plains region which the settlers had to cross, however, the situation was different. Here, the arrival—with the White people—of guns and horses had given rise to the last great flowering of free North American Indian culture. Bands that had made a living by hunting bison on foot, and semi-agricultural tribes from the eastern plains or further east still, had taken to roaming in mounted bands across the vast grasslands of the American west in pursuit of buffalo herds.

It did not take them long to quickly evolve a highly efficient way of life, giving them plentiful food, complex cultures and all the accoutrements that were later to become the hallmarks of the Hollywood Red Man: huge feather warbonnets, coup-sticks, large skin *tipis*, pipes and pony-herds. Increasing pressures from other tribes, driven by Whites on to the Plains, meant that these peoples had to exist almost permanently on a war footing, developing efficient military societies and a heroic warrior ethos, but despite all difficulties they flourished for about a hundred years. Then the Whites started to arrive in numbers.

At first the Americans only asked for access, but friction quickly developed and hostilities escalated, both sides acting, as they saw it, in self-defence. Clashes between Sioux and Cheyennes on the one hand, and settlers and soldiers moving west and disturbing the vital buffalo herds on the other, occurred sporadically through the 1850s. In 1862, during the American Civil War, there was an uprising of Eastern Sioux in Minnesota, where the Indians had been seriously abused by local Whites and Government officials. The trouble spread west into the Dakotas and volunteer troops from the frontier states and territories moved in, eager to confront the Indians if a full-scale war broke out. Inevitably, tension heightened.

Serious fighting broke out between the Americans and the Sioux, Cheyennes, Arapahos, Kiowas, Comanches and others, and feeling against the Indian quickly hardened. The Plains tribes were fighting so skilfully and courageously for their land that the cost of killing them worked out at a million dollars per dead Indian. At the same time, the basis for American policy was the now widely-held belief that the Redskin was doomed by the 'march of progress', and the fact that the forces of 'progress' were being so signally unsuccessful at clearing him out of the way was both disquieting and humiliating.

More extreme measures seemed justified. In 1871, General E. C. Walker,

Charles Herbert

Commissioner of Indian Affairs, expressed the White view: 'When dealing with savage men, as with savage beasts, no questions of national honour can arise. Whether to fight, to run away, or to employ a ruse is solely a matter of expediency.'

In the same year Congress decided to stop treating with the Indians as independent nations and at about the same time a new policy was instigated: the Indians would be starved off the Plains by the wholesale destruction of the buffalo herds on which they lived. This scheme was extremely effective; in the middle of the 19th century there were 60 million or so North American bison, and by the beginning of the 20th there were ten left.

In 1874 the discovery of gold in the Black Hills of South Dakota, which the Sioux regarded as sacred and had retained under the treaty of 1868, led to a Gold Rush. The Indians would not sell the Hills; they threatened war and when the Government ordered them on to reservations large numbers refused to move. In March 1876 General George Crook was sent with a large force to round them up and three months later one of his columns, led by Colonel Custer, attacked an encampment of Sioux and Cheyennes on the Little Bighorn River.

Two hundred and twenty-five of the Americans were killed; the rest fled. The United States was deeply shocked, and efforts against the Indians were redoubled. Harrassed by troops, and driven to starvation by the extermination of the bison, the Plains Indians were gradually forced on to the reservations, their numbers drastically depleted.

Elsewhere in America the final defeat of the free tribes was being accomplished: in 1879 Chief Joseph and his Nez Perces surrendered in the northwest, in 1886 the Apache leader Geronimo at last gave himself up, and an uprising in the Canadian west was suppressed. The last defiant hopes of the Indians concentrated on a messianic cult which promised that by taking part in a Ghost Dance the Plains tribes would bring back the buffalo and their own dead people. In 1890, at Wounded Knee, South Dakota, US troops grew nervy at the fervent emotion generated by the dance and massacred 300 Sioux. It was the last major military action against the Indians in the United States.

The battle against Indian culture and 'Indianness' nonetheless continued. On reservations that generally consisted of the poorest land and were too small to support them, the remains of the tribes were administered by cumbrous bureaucracies determined to solve the 'Indian Problem'. Throughout this century opinions about what exactly the problem

is, and what should be done about it, have changed from administration to administration, with the result that the Indians, already trying to understand what an alien world requires of them, are still more confused by the variety of advice and instruction that they receive.

In the meantime, while different approaches have been tried and found wanting, the Indians have been kept alive, usually in considerable poverty and cut off from the rest of American society. They have become dependent on welfare payments which cost the government less than developing employment opportunities near centres of Indian population.

Whatever methods they suggest, government policies have with one or two notable exceptions been founded on the assumption that Indians can ultimately succeed in modern North America only if they cease to be Indian and are totally assimilated into the dominant society. There have been persistent efforts, by education and other means, to discredit the values and attitudes of traditional native cultures, which have been dismissed as superstitious and totally irrelevant to the realities of the 20th century.

The notion of tribal, as opposed to personal, property has been undermined, most devastatingly by the Dawes Act of 1887, which provided for the 'allotment' of land to individual Indians, who were then empowered to sell it. In this way, during the 47 years of the Act's life, Indian holdings of land in the United States fell from some 56 million ha (138 million acres) to 20 million ha (50 million acres).

The first and most wholehearted reversal of assimilationist policy came in 1933, when President Roosevelt appointed John Collier, a sociologist and a passionate admirer of native cultures, as Commissioner for Indian Affairs. Collier believed that the Indians could best cope with the modern world from a secure base of their own land and government. Under the Indian Reorganization Act of 1934, power was channelled away from the bureaucracy and back to the Indians on the reservations, allotment was prohibited and a range of human and economic resources was put at the disposal of native communities. In 1945, at the end of Collier's tenure of office, the combined effects of the Depression and the Second World War had worked to minimize the changes this policy had been designed to bring about.

Under the Eisenhower régime the official approach was again to encourage the termination of the special relationship between Indian and federal government, to divide up land-holdings and give the native a status identical with that of other Americans. But the consequences of this policy on the groups who accepted 'termination' were so disastrous that it

was halted again. All the problems of drunkenness, delinquency, cultural and emotional maladjustment, unemployment and discrimination which had beset reservation life were intensified enormously when large quantities of Indians, untrained and poorly educated, descended on the cities and started trying to compete with Whites for jobs. It became clear that to talk of equal opportunity for people who set out so handicapped was a nonsense.

Since the 1950s there have been attempts, both in the US and Canada, to improve reservation life so that the Indians have a firmer base on which to stand while trying to adjust to the outside world; but despite this they remain the most depressed and poorest ethnic minorities in both countries, with unemployment often running at over 50 per cent and incomes a fraction of the national averages. The situation is exacerbated by the fact that with improved medical services the number of people with enough native blood or culture to be regarded as Indian is rapidly increasing, and in the United States and Canada combined already probably exceeds one million.

Although many of these do not depend on reservations or tribal membership for their livelihoods, it is clear that the land, which was distributed by conquering governments at a period when Indian population was at its lowest, has since been greatly diminished and is completely inadequate to cope with the needs of the Indian today. Another difficulty is that administrations with a four-year life-span and an eye always on the next election have consistently underrated the time and money necessary for radical improvements.

Nonetheless, the Indians themselves, partly under the influence of Civil Rights and Black Power movements, have been organizing and lobbying far more effectively the past years. Organizations like the militant American Indian Movement and the more moderate, but powerful and effective, National Indian Brotherhood in Canada, have publicized many of the problems and attracted support on a pan-Indian, inter-tribal basis.

Perhaps as important in some ways has been the growing interest of non-Indians in a native culture. As the simplistic Victorian idea of endless material progress comes to seem increasingly implausible, many people feel that the Indians who have stubbornly held to their own traditions—particularly those concerning tribal society and attitudes to nature—can offer preferable and more useful values, and that the adaptations they evolved over thousands of years may be more appropriate to America than many of the technologies transplanted from Europe. □

Africa: Yesterday and Tomorrow

The newly independent states of Black Africa still bear the unmistakable imprint of Europe in many ways—their national boundaries, their political structures, their educational and legal systems, and above all their official languages. As a result of the imposition of colonial rule, Africans were forced to accept much of European culture which they might otherwise have rejected.

In asserting their political independence from the European imperial powers, African states also stressed the need to establish their own cultural identities. But they did not seek cultural isolation. Rather they looked back to the freedom exercised by pre-colonial African states which could choose freely those aspects of foreign cultures they would accept and those they would reject.

The Nigerian artist Uche Okeke put the position nicely in a speech he made on the eve of Nigerian Independence in 1960: 'We must fight to free ourselves from mirroring foreign culture . . . we must have our own school of art independent of European and Oriental schools, but drawing, as much as possible, from what we consider in our clear judgement to be the cream of these influences and welding them to our native art culture.'

Meeting as Equals

Africa has a long and complex history and contact between African and other cultures had been going on for many thousands of years before the arrival of the Europeans. It is possible that humans originated in Africa: certainly many of the most important technological advances of the Stone Age were made there.

Thus for most of our long history, Africa was probably an 'exporter' of cultural ideas. In more recent times, and particularly under the influence of the Arabs and later, the Europeans, Africans have played a more passive role: they have been on the 'receiving end' of the process of cultural exchange. But the process has always been one of inter-reaction and it is a mistake to think that it was ever entirely 'one way'.

Throughout their history Africans have shown a remarkably high capacity for adaptation and absorption of imported technology and ideas. Change has taken place, and at times the changes

have caused considerable social disruption, but total collapse has rarely resulted.

Up to the eve of the European invasion of Africa at the end of the 19th century, Africans dealt with Europeans and Moslem Arabs as equals. When they accepted elements of the cultures of these peoples, it was not as a result of force. The impact of European culture before colonial rule had been negligible compared with that of the Moslems.

Whilst initially the Portuguese had explored the west coast of Africa with evangelical as well as commercial motives, their concern with converting African kings to Christianity soon waned in the face of the profits to be made from the slave trade. Only in Benin, Warri and the Kongo were Christian missions established, and these were all short-lived. While the King of Kongo was converted and his successor learnt to read and write, and sought technical assistance from the Portuguese, the latter's greed for slaves decimated and devastated his kingdom which soon abandoned the new found Christianity.

The impact of the Portuguese and other European slave traders in Africa was for the most part negative. For slaves and gold, European traders exchanged liquor, cloths, salt, dried fish, iron bars, copper, brass, cowrie-shells and guns. With the exception of the last four all these items were produced locally. So African life was not culturally or materially enriched in any important way.

Africa's only technological gain was the acquisition of guns which were the principal instrument of prosecuting the wars by which slaves were obtained. The price was of course over 8,500,000 Africans, at the prime of their life, shipped across the Atlantic and countless millions more, killed in the slave-capturing wars.

In the first three and a half centuries of contact between Africa and Europe, few Africans learnt how to read and write, let alone anything of European education. By 1807, when Britain abolished the slave trade, Europe had left little or no cultural mark on the African societies with which she traded. This contrasts dramatically with the much more extensive impact of Arab culture as the three centuries of contact between the Hausa States of Kano and Katsina and the Arabs during the same period showed.

Trade across the desert between North Africa and the Hausa states did not really open up until the 15th century. Islam had percolated through to both Kano and Katsina as a result of trade with Wangara merchants from Mali and with Kanem-Bornu, both already deeply involved in the trans-Saharan trade.

By the time the trans-Saharan trade had become important for Kano and Katsina, both their kings, Mohammed Rumfa and Mohammed Korau, had become Moslems. Not only did they adopt the religion of the Arab traders but they sought advice from a distinguished Moslem jurist, Al-Maghili, as to how they should run their governments according to Moslem law. For them, he wrote a treatise, subsequently translated into English as *The Obligations of Princes*.

Impact of Islam

Islam had, of course, long since become an important factor on the east coast of Africa and in some other states of the Western and Central Sudan of which the Arabs had already opened up trade: Ghana, its successor Mali, and Kanem-Bornu. Arab trade with Kano and Katsina began at roughly the same time as European trade began with West Africa, yet the cultural impact of the two sets of traders was totally different.

Despite the proximity of the European ports to the capital of the Asante Empire, the Asantehene, Osei Kojo (1764–77), employed literate Moslem Africans in his chancery, not literate Christian Africans as there were none available. While Africans adopted the religion of the Arab traders and its adjuncts of literacy, a legal system and system of government, the Europeans made negligible cultural impact.

Islam had a profound effect on the whole of the Sudanic belt across Africa south of the Sahara. However, it never penetrated the forest region, partly because the forest was unsuited to the pastoralist economy which often came with it. It is also true that the peoples of the forest had developed strongly integrated cultures. In these, each aspect of social organization and belief depended on the adoption of all other 'foreign ideas'—political, economic and religious.

In the savannah, by contrast, there were often rulers strong enough to impose a new religion, at least at the court, and they had additional motives for doing so. They needed literate teachers who could help as administrators and judges in running the state.

In the Hausa states the Islamic religion was sufficiently implanted over 300 years to provoke a *jihad* or holy war by devout Moslems against rulers whom they accused of not governing their people according to the *Sharia* (the Islamic law). The extent of the learning that backed up this attempt at reform is amply demonstrated by the writings of its leader, the Shehu Usman dan Fodio, his brother Abdullahi, and his son, the Caliph Muhammad Bello.

By 1800 only a few isolated Africans had, by contrast, adopted Christianity and Western education. Christianity was influential only in enclaves round European trading posts in West Africa or settlements in South Africa. Traditional rulers might have absorbed European goods like umbrellas into their 'traditional' regalia. None of them were converted, however, to Christianity.

With the evangelical offensive of the 19th century, the abolitionist movement and the penetration of freed slaves from the coastal enclaves into the interior—followed by missionaries, traders, explorers, consuls and later governors—it seemed that European cultural influences

might begin to rival those of Moslem Arabia. The volume and the coverage of European trade spread rapidly and freed slaves proved very effective proselytizers for European culture.

Nevertheless, there was no wholesale adoption of European cultural and spiritual values comparable to those of Islam. Africans still dealt with European missionaries and traders as well as their freed-slave agents on a basis of moral equality. Some of their rulers began cautiously to seek after Western education as a way of gaining something of European technology but they hoped to adopt such technology only within the context of their own traditional cultures.

Conquest and Colonialism

The colonial period changed all that. Based on technological superiority firmly established on the battlefield, the Europeans assumed not merely a military right to rule but also a moral superiority which entitled them to mould Africa according to his own design. Many Africans

S.W.A.P.O.

A genteel Gold Coast croquet party in the 1870s had both Black and White guests. Before the scramble for Africa and the arrival of permanent settlers, both Europeans and Moslem Arabs had dealt with Africans as equals.

These two Herero were captured by the Germans in Namibia. The only Herero to survive were those who fled when the colonists launched a policy of genocide which reduced their numbers from 90,000 to 20,000 in just six months of 1904.

Popperfoto

As Henry Stanley, Daily Telegraph correspondent and explorer, filled in details of the map of Central Africa so adventurers, missionaries, administrators and exploiters followed in his wake. Africa would never be the same again.

lost not only their sovereignty and freedom of choice, but also their self-confidence and cultural orientation.

The Africans, whether they liked it or not, had to deal with the alien institutions of the colonial ruler. Many of these, like their legal system, became unavoidable channels for transmitting European culture. Though direct European cultural influence was uneven, eventually every part of the continent was brought into the sphere of colonial exploitation either by direct contribution of labour, cash crops, mining or agricultural land, or at the least by the payment of taxes.

Every European was protected by the power and prestige of the ruling race. The white *bwana* was 'sacred' and no one was allowed to take advantage of his human weaknesses. Personal injury to one of them could lead to the wiping out of a whole African village. This meant that all African peoples were made to feel the sense of conquest and loss of sovereignty and forced to recognize the superiority of the White people's world.

A radio and a Swahili newspaper symbolize a transformation in the horizons of Africa's middle class. For the first time Africans have developed an interest in the whole continent and are adopting a non-tribal identity.

No people were so remote that they did not become aware of the wider world outside. Their own world, however exclusive hitherto, had been broken into. As the Yoruba put it: '*Aiye d'aiye Oyinbo*—the world has become a White man's world'. New psychological and even religious adjustments had to be made to this new situation.

British administration policies of ruling where possible through the existing indigenous authorities—Indirect Rule—were ostensibly intended to disturb the traditional world view of the colonial subjects, 'Protected Persons', as little as possible.

However, the very presence of the colonial authority presiding over previously sovereign peoples created a new situation. The British power to appoint and depose chiefs, to turn them into tax-collectors and to set up courts enforcing British-made laws, were all aspects of a new and revolutionary situation.

The French and the Portuguese made little pretence of trying to minimize the effects of such interventions in their subjects' lives. They divided states and amalgamated others in a deliberate attempt to rationalize the units of administration and absorb the territories as permanent parts of the metropolitan countries.

The power to divide an autonomous

state or to amalgamate it with others within new administrative units was one of the most far-reaching interventions in the historical development of African peoples. It made much more of a lasting impact on the cultural values of Africa than the attempts to bring a handful of the African elite under the direct cultural influence of Europe. That the cultural defences of Africans did not crumble was due largely to the adaptability and resilience of their cultures.

After the initial trauma of colonial subjugation, many African communities recovered some self-confidence. They found that Europeans were thinly spread on the ground and could not be everywhere at the same time. During the First World War when the French were weak in West Africa with the withdrawal of so

many of their administrators and traders to the European front, there were widescale revolts by Africans seeking to regain the independence they had so recently lost.

Europeans were so ignorant of the inner workings of African societies that they could often be ignored, avoided or outwitted, especially in the rural areas. It is against this background that the impact of different aspects of the European colonial presence should be evaluated.

Foreign Gods

Conversion to Christianity was envisaged by many Europeans as the principal means of creating a new person out of the African and ensuring the cultural domination of Europe.

Many African rulers recognized

Christianity as a subversive force and tried to keep it at a safe distance. So great was the prestige of the Whites that many people were inevitably attracted to their religion as a possible key to understanding their success. Cautiously at first, and then in larger numbers, Africans accepted the Christian way of life.

But conversion was usually less than total. The converted African was, in theory, to cease being a member of his traditional community since he should no longer believe in the old gods, venerate the ancestors or respect the sanctions that previously held the community together.

In the event, Christianity has not proved as revolutionary as its portent, and the influence of Europe on African culture and values cannot be evaluated simply by the statistics of Africans claiming to be Christians. Nonetheless the considerable material benefits brought by hospitals and schools testify to Christianity's impact.

The total rejection of African culture and values demanded by 19th century missionaries from African converts has not been realized. The Churches continue to inveigh against Christians marrying a plurality of wives, believing in witches or placing their faith in traditional charms.

These are but overt indications that many Christians have tried to adapt aspects of Christian teaching to their values and cultural environment. They have also sometimes tried to add the Christian God to their traditional pantheon. As much as some converts believe many Christian teachings they continue in their daily lives to be guided by traditional values.

Indeed, many of the causes missionaries fought for were won not through a change of heart among the converted but as a result of the effects of secular European activities. Thus, whatever success missionary crusades against polygamy, slavery, the murder of twins, and trial by ordeal achieved, was finally won only through the laws of the colonial administrators. In other areas such as the belief in witches and adherence to the traditional ideas of the causation of disease, the expansion of hospitals and Western education have done more than the Churches to discredit the traditional order.

The limitations of the cultural impact achieved by the European missionary churches in Africa are highlighted by the increasing proliferation and great influence of separatist African Churches.

Foto Hetzel

Schoolchildren are still taught French in independent Benin where it is the lingua franca. In the past Africans learnt much more about the culture of France, Britain or Portugal than their own.

In many cases, these have been more ruthless and more successful in the crusade against the old gods and beliefs.

But they have not been willing to go along with the official missionary Churches from Europe in demanding total rejection of African culture and values. They incorporate into their worship and liturgies elements of traditional religion and practice such as drumming, possession, belief in multiple spirits, and even witches, as well as the traditional explanations of the social and environmental causes of illness and healing.

In spite of the prestige attaching to the title of Christian in colonial times, there are still more non-Christians than Christians in Black Africa, and also more Moslems than Christians. Indeed, Islam made more headway under colonial rule than ever it did before. Not being identified as a White man's religion, or as the religion of the colonial rulers, and having been indigenized over so many centuries, it gained many converts among those uprooted from their traditional life.

With the improvement of communications, and in particular the opening of air-routes to Saudi Arabia, the Holy Pilgrimage or *Hajj* to Mecca has opened up the Islamized areas of Africa to powerful influences—both cultural and political —from the Moslem and Arab worlds.

Trade Follows the Flag
The European commercial community probably disrupted the life of colonized Africans more than did the missionaries. There is not too much exaggeration in the common saying, that while the missionaries directed the people's eyes heavenward, the commercial community carried away their property. And while it was easier to avoid missionary preaching, the new order was more difficult to side-step.

European powers in Africa followed a policy of *laissez-faire* in matters affecting the well-being of the peasants, but openly intervened to promote the interests of their own commercial community. It is therefore in this area that the term colonial exploitation becomes most appropriate in describing the relationship between Africa and Europe in the colonial period.

Colonial administrators were concerned mainly with the encouragement of cash crops and the exploitation of minerals. Little attention was paid to the production of food crops. The various administrations also built ports and developed roads and railways to the areas in the interior where the cash crops and minerals were located.

Colonial regimes can claim little credit for improving by direct policies the economies or standard of living of their territories. They forced the peasantry into the world economy as dependent parts of the metropolitan economies.

European rulers introduced currencies tied to their own currencies and introduced direct taxation as a means of inducing the peasants to work in plantations, mines, or to produce crops. Some instituted forced labour, fixed low wages, and recruited labour for European firms. By such means and through control of banking, currency, shipping and customs, the economies of colonial Africa were maintained in the firm grip of the European mercantile communities.

The colonial economy was thus one in which the wealth of Africa continuously flowed out. The imports were mostly substitutes for locally manufactured goods, which often destroyed traditional crafts and manufactures. The result was moderate well-being in the areas where cash crops were grown and consequent

migrations of peasants to them as well as to the mines and the new coastal cities where the European firms were located.

These developments clearly disrupted traditional patterns of society and communal relationships. The cash nexus replaced many traditional social obligations to the distortion of the social values of those relationships. The money economy has sharpened the differences between social classes in terms of the material possessions, houses and pattern of family life, and the values placed on these things.

Nevertheless, the majority of Africans continue to subsist by traditional exchange and carry on developing their own domestic economies based on internal distribution networks, whether comple-

Larry Herman

(Above) A Tanzanian mechanic services an engine chosen for its low cost and easy maintenance. Until recently much of Africa accepted foreign technology without questioning its cost.

(Below) Indian films are popular in West Africa as well as in East Africa where 250,000 Asians have settled. Africa has yet to develop its own film industry and a recent foreign film obsession was Kung Fu.

Mike Andrews

Bruno Barbey/Magnum

(Left) West African lawyers in particular have adopted many features of European legal systems. Besides the costume, fundamental Western concepts of law and justice have been retained by Africa.

(Right) Malian Moslems worship Allah at the Mopti mosque. Today the influence of Islam continues to spread southwards in West Africa and there are increasingly more Moslems than Christians.

mented or not be the new coast to hinterland roads and railways of the colonial regimes.

Domination of Africans by Europeans was underlined by their legal systems. A principal pre-occupation of the colonial administration was to maintain law and order. They did this by setting up new systems of justice over the traditional systems. Various forms of combinations of European-type courts and native or customary courts were established.

Taking the British colonies as an example, the general predominance of the foreign over the local system was ensured by the application of the doctrine of repugnancy: that is, that African laws and customs might be accepted as valid only in so far as they were not repugnant to 'principles of natural justice, equity and good conscience'.

By the simple application of the doctrine of repugnancy, several local customary usages were outlawed. In such formal aspects of the legal system as the law of evidence and procedure, too, the European model has tended to override traditional ways in most of Africa—except perhaps in those areas where Moslem law is practised. European law also predominates in the commercial and industrial sphere where it facilitated the extraction of Africa's wealth.

The areas in which the different attitudes of Europe and Africa become most significant to the majority of Africans are probably those laws that regulate marriage, land tenure, and inheritance. The common African traditions of poly-

A Kenyan couple are married in a Christian church. Today many Africans who call themselves Christians have not abandoned completely their old beliefs, practices and gods.

gymy and communal ownership of land had to contend with the Europeans' ideas of monogamy and individual ownership. Various devices have been worked out in the legal systems to encourage European preferences for the patrilineal and monogamous family.

But here again, many individuals have simply gone their own ways with scant regard for the official legal pronouncements. For example, the provision of the Nigerian law that a man who has married one wife 'according to the ordinance' in Church or in a Registry, can no longer marry other wives by local tradition, is broken daily without much social disapproval. Similarly, large numbers of rural people continue to settle their domestic, land, and other disputes in traditional and informal ways without recourse to the official courts.

However, some lawyers and elite rulers of the new African states welcome as

Marion Kaplan

salutary the unifying function of the European models. They also readily accept the sweeping away of certain traditional practices by the principle of repugnancy. Nevertheless, it is clear that in spite of the powerful patronage that European legal systems have received, and such major inroads as they have made into customary laws and usages, Africans' views of what genuinely constitutes crime and anti-social behaviour are still largely governed by concepts and values from traditional cultures.

Learning and Unlearning

Schools have proved far more potent culturally than Churches, if only because they are directed at the more impressionable youth. The need for commercial intercourse with Europe, access to jobs under the colonial system and the modernizing sectors of society, the desire to imitate the powerful and prestigious Europeans—all these induced parents to send children to school.

For all the attempt of parents and societies to erect cultural barriers to protect the cultures of their youth, Western education has had a powerful impact on them. Most educated young people learn to lose faith in the old gods, though they seldom completely cease to fear that evil forces can still be manipulated against them. They learn to accept many European social and cultural ideas. No longer do they have the time or the opportunity to learn enough about their traditional society to understand fully the basis of its culture and philosophy.

If the colonial regimes had in fact been able to push Western education vigorously, they would indeed have made a significant impact on African cultures and values. However, they had too little money to devote to education and were content for the most part to leave education in the hands of missionaries who tended to see schools largely from the point of view of evangelization.

The result was that the number and coverage of schools was small, though their products came to exercise political, social and economic influence far beyond their numbers. Further, few of the products of the schools were sufficiently well

Georg Gerster/John Hillelson Agency

political, commercial and cultural offensives in Africa, exposing its peoples to ideas from the New World, the Communist World and the Orient.

The mass media, so rapidly developed since independence, carrying programmes from all over the world. In Nigeria young people avidly watch Indian and Chinese films, and one popular fashion for decorating 'mammy-wagons' is a picture of two young men engaged in the art of Kung Fu. While colonial rule enlarged the world horizons of many African societies it did not integrate Africans into the modern world, only that part of it in which the particular colonial power was involved.

A New Identity

With independence, African states have entered fully into the world community and are subject to all its various political, cultural and economic pressures. More important from having been predominantly on the receiving end as far as cultural contact was concerned during the period of colonial rule, today the old myths of the inferiority of African culture have been shattered.

African culture, both traditional and modern, is having an impact on the wider world: the political ideas of Amilcar Cabral and Julius Nyerere or the writings of Wole Soyinka and Leopold Sedar Senghor are internationally known.

Yet it remains true to say that as the people of Namibia and South Africa struggle to overthrow the last bastion of European rule on the continent, European impact has so far been the greatest outside influence on contemporary Africa. But as in the past when the Arab influence was so important, there is little ground for suggesting that there has been a wholesale collapse of African culture and values as a result of European contact.

No one can deny the great changes that have resulted from colonial domination, European missionary indoctrination, and the exploitation of African economic and mineral resources. Indeed, the changes that have taken place after African countries have regained their political independence may be judged even more far-reaching and significant than the changes of the colonial era. For this reason it may be premature to attempt any definitive statement of the impact of Europe on Africa as the process has not come to an end, it may even be accelerating.

Africa is now right in the middle of the process of adapting and adopting new ideas, technologies and skills. What is more, the values and ideas which Africans are now striving to acquire have become the property of the whole world, and it is difficult to demarcate them as influences distinctly European any more.

educated to fill the cultural vacuum created in their minds by an inadequate comprehension of European cultural values.

There was in consequence a good deal of residual African values that life in African society and interaction with non-literate rural peoples did not fail to reinforce. Thus, as in the case of conversion, Western education was seldom as successful in implanting European cultural values as exaggerated pictures of the disruptive influences of Western education would suggest. Above all, the tiny educated minority, whatever their political, social and economic power, remained culturally very dependent on the vast majority.

The regaining of political independence has restored freedom of choice to Africans. This has not meant a wholesale rejection of European culture: rather while African political and cultural leaders have talked much in terms of re-establishing the cultural identity of their people, of Négritude and the African personality, European influences have continued unabated. If anything, they have become stronger since the wave of independence swept through most of Africa in the 1950s and 1960s.

Whereas under colonial rule African countries were subject largely to the influence of the particular European power that had colonized them, now they have diplomatic, commercial and cultural relations with a much wider range of them. More than that, the United States, and to a lesser extent the Soviet Union, China and Japan, have begun

Future for Aboriginal Peoples

In December 1967 a band of 16 Cuiva Indians accepted an invitation to a meal at the La Rubiela ranch near the border of Colombia and Venezuela. When they arrived they were killed by their hosts. During the trial which followed, the ranchers admitted the crime, and also the slaughter of another 40 or so Indians in similar exploits, but were acquitted on the grounds that, like most of the Whites in the area, they did not consider the Cuiva human and thus did not regard killing them as murder. The case created a national and international scandal, but attacks on the Indians and encroachments on their territory have continued. Today there are fewer than 500 Cuiva left, divided among three bands.

It would be impossible to assess accurately how many peoples and cultures have been totally or partially destroyed over the past five centuries, or how many are threatened today. The UN Sub-Commission on the Prevention of Discrimination and Protection of Minorities has recently been attempting to form a reliable estimate of the numbers and situations of indigenous groups throughout the world, but its efforts have so far been frustrated. Many governments are reluctant even to admit that they have a distinct aboriginal population and

Amahuaca children in Peru parade for a nun at the Christian mission. Although missionaries have often tried to protect aboriginals, they have also attacked their traditional cultures with foreign values.

others refuse to answer questions at all.

An informed guess, however, suggests that there may be as many as 10,000,000 people living in small, autonomous or semi-autonomous tribal societies who are in immediate grave danger of 'colonization'—which effectively means a foreign invasion of their territory, the death of most or all of their members and a wretched and demoralised existence for any survivors—by members of the more populous, and culturally dissimilar, nation states that surround them.

The seeds of these problems all lie in the history of Europe over the past 500 years. Towards the close of the Middle Ages, when Europe's essentially self-contained feudal system was collapsing, a new merchant economy, based on unequal exchange between the producers of raw materials and the manufacturers of finished goods, became increasingly important and there was a growing need for new suppliers and markets. Over the next 200 years a trading network was

gradually established first with America, and then with the peoples of coastal Africa, parts of Asia, Australia and the Pacific.

Increasingly, however, the situation became dominated by White people's hunger for land. The success of overseas enterprises and the exhaustion of the resources of region after region had created an ever-growing demand for markets and materials. This in turn stimulated a series of inventions that widened the technological gulf between Europeans and aboriginal peoples. Ceaseless expansion and more and more efficient exploitation were now possible, and increasing numbers of Whites sought not only economic opportunities but also a permanent home in the newly-discovered continents.

The natives, even if they adapted their traditional way of life, were of decreasing use to the settlers. Their existence was tolerated only if they accepted a servile position in the colonial economy and assisted in the exploitation of their own land and resources. Every continent was touched by this problem to some extent, but it was America that felt the effects first and was most tragically transformed. Between the end of the 15th century and the end of the 19th, Britons, Spaniards,

2662

Disappearing World/Granada Television

(Above) The Cuiva Indians of Colombia now number less than 500 and are under growing threat of extinction. As their lands are reduced, they become dependent on the White settlers around them.

(Right) The frontier settlers have little understanding of the Cuiva, whom they regard as lazy and unproductive. Now many Indians have been forced to work as labourers on their farms, for very low wages.

Disappearing World/Granada Television

Portuguese and their descendants spread out relentlessly and engulfed the entire Western Hemisphere, destroying as they did so many millions of native people and reducing the Indian population to between 10 and 20 per cent of its probable pre-Columbian level.

Wherever this process of dispossession has taken place and continues to take place, it has followed a remarkably similar pattern. With the exception of the Inca and Aztec empires, which perished very early on, indigenous societies have tended by European standards to be small, self-sufficient, technologically primitive units, and their response to the colonial experience has been shaped by certain widely-shared values and characteristics. Moreover, the cultural and physical qualities of the people making the initial contacts with aboriginal groups have remained fairly constant.

In many cases, European illnesses, transmitted through other native peoples, move ahead of the first actual meetings, decimating the population and leaving the survivors demoralised, terrified and bewildered by what appears to be a bout of terrible supernatural anger. These conditions make it easier for traders and missionaries to gain a foothold when they arrive. The weakened natives gladly accept presents of food, medicine and implements, especially iron tools and weapons, which are usually more efficient than their indigenous counterparts. These innovations often lead to enormous material benefits in the short-term, bringing unprecedented prosperity and modifying native societies.

Such advantages are only temporary, however, Once the self-sufficiency of the tribe is broken, so that it can no longer subsist entirely with its own artefacts and by its own efforts, the trader uses his monopoly position to extort higher and higher payments in goods and labour for the ammunition and other necessaries he provides. This system, used by the Hudson's Bay Company in Canada and widely practised among the forest and mountain tribes of South America and elsewhere, quickly leaves the native in a state of permanent debt, forced to ask for more supplies to enable him to work off the cost of the last consignment.

During the next phase, advance parties of settlers and fortune-seekers follow the traders into the region. By now the aboriginal group lacks independent resources to resist the mounting pressure on its land. When violence breaks out between native and frontiersman the government, although probably in theory recognising the tribe's right to at least some of its land, claims either that it is powerless to act or that there has been 'an atrocity' which justifies its intervention on behalf of the settlers.

After a series of clashes, in which the more numerous and better-armed newcomers are almost invariably triumphant, they impose progressively harsher conditions on the native. The tribespeople are then either driven from the region altogether—in which case they have merely postponed their eventual destruction—or, virtually landless and much diminished in number, lose the means and the social coherence to subsist by their traditional methods.

In Australia and North America it has been customary for such people to be established on reservations or in mission settlements where they can be kept alive at a very basic level and trained to despise their own culture and adopt that of the

2663

Whites. In this way, it has been supposed they will disappear as a separate people, either dying off or being assimilated into the 'melting-pot'. In South America and Asia it has been more usual to leave agricultural tribes in their villages and exploit them economically either as landless labourers or through the debt system, while nomadic or migratory bands have generally been forced into the settlers' towns and villages. There, if they survive at all, they will ultimately be absorbed into the lowest segment of the dominant society.

This process of destruction has now been completed throughout most of the colonised world, but in some of the more remote areas of South America, Africa, Asia, the Pacific and elsewhere it is still in its early stages—and today, despite its European origins, is often being carried out by non-Europeans. All the indications suggest, however, that those peoples who have not yet succumbed completely will be overwhelmed in the very near future.

The television documentary 'A Decade of Destruction', shown in the U.K. in January 1984 gave a clear picture of how the way of life of the Amazonian Indians was inevitably destroyed in the path of 'developing' the area, in spite of efforts to protect their rights.

From the beginning, and particularly over the past two centuries, Europeans have maintained that the fate of indigenous peoples was inevitable. In the early stages, this belief stemmed from the notion that history had been pre-ordained—in White people's favour—by the one true Christian God. Later, in the 19th century, technological innovation seemed to be giving Europe complete mastery of the world and there was a growing faith in the superiority of the Western intellect—the theories of men such as Darwin

and Marx suggested that this pre-determination came from the principles of nature.

This concept, in diluted form, became commonplace in the widespread idea of 'Progress' as an irresistible evolutionary force which condemned outmoded human societies just as, 65 million years before, it had condemned the outmoded dinosaur. Its next victim would be the superstitious, backward, inefficient and ignorant primitive—the Savage, whether Noble or Brutal, would inevitably be destroyed by, or absorbed in, a worldwide society based on the European pattern and enjoying unending technical, economic and social advances.

In recent years this assumption has been challenged in Europe and North America by a small but growing body of people. One reason is that, contrary to expectation, groups such as the North American Indians have failed to disappear. Tribes such as the Pueblos and the Navajos, who until this century were comparatively isolated from outside influence, are still intact and to a large degree independent. On the east coast of the United States, small but identifiable communities of people, for example the Passamaquoddies—who according to the history books had been destroyed before the end of the 17th century—can still be found, fiercely proclaiming their 'Indianness' and often preserving their languages and elements of their ancient cultures.

The fact that such people have survived and continue to struggle against enormous odds to keep themselves distinct from a dominant society has created unforeseen problems for governments whose aboriginal policies were conceived and implemented hastily on the assumption that native people would simply vanish. The United States, for instance, gave pitifully inadequate tracts of the most worthless land to its Indians in the last century and has since been trying to reduce the reservations still further. Now it must spend over $1,000 million annually just to maintain some 600,000 native people as the poorest and

most troubled ethnic group in the country. This should serve as a warning to other governments who are attempting to solve their 'aboriginal problem' with short-term, cut-price solutions that will eventually prove far more expensive, in both human and financial terms, than allowing the indigenous tribes to keep their territory and their self-sufficiency.

Another factor in the changing attitude towards aboriginal people has been the growing weight of expert opinion that the scientific and economic premises of the argument for 'boundless progress' are pure fantasy. It now seems clear that if current trends continue unchecked they will create not a materialist Utopia but an exhausted, polluted dustbowl without the resources to support either its technology or its vast and hungry population.

Aboriginal societies are not merely the victims of this situation, they may offer the only viable alternatives to it. For five centuries Westerners have been evolving techniques for dominating, exploiting and ultimately impoverishing every area of the world—trying to adapt the environment permanently to themselves without respect for the life and special potentials of each locality. Meanwhile, indigenous peoples—in the few places where they still exist relatively undisturbed—have been continuing the gradual process of adapting themselves more and more efficiently to their environments.

The difference between these two approaches is philosophical as well as technological. In contrast to Europeans, with their obsession with historical change, aboriginals tend to be relatively uninterested in linear time. They concern themselves instead with a pattern of behaviour, ordained 'at the beginning' by some mythological hero or deity and renewed with only minor variations year

Claudio Villas Boas takes the temperature of a Xingu Indian in a protected area of Brazil. Many aboriginal groups have been decimated by European diseases, to which they have no immunity.

The Andoke Indians of Colombia have set up an independent co-operative to extract and sell rubber themselves. This project, and the equipment necessary, was initially funded by Survival International.

after year. This pattern enables them to subsist efficiently at every season balance and harmony with their human and natural surroundings.

In this way indigenous societies have for countless generations received, improved and passed on knowledge and understanding of their particular environments which far surpass those of the 'modern world'. They have evolved techniques for surviving and for harvesting the local food-supplies that probably offer—in many cases at least—the most efficient, and perhaps the only, long-term way of supporting human life in their areas.

The knowledge that indigenous peoples have, or could have, contributed in this field is suggested by the fact that almost half the crops at present under cultivation throughout the world were first grown by the comparatively small pre-Columbian population of the Americas. They also possessed an extraordinarily comprehensive pharmacoepia that has benefited Western medicine enormously. Every time an aboriginal society is swept out of the path of 'Progress' the information and skills that it has developed over hundreds or thousands of years of painstaking experiment and adjustment dies with it. This is a loss which the modern world quite simply cannot afford.

It is ironic that at the moment when Western Europe and North America are beginning to appreciate the value and importance of aboriginal groups, the assumptions and policies of 19th century Europe are still being practised—frequently by people who are not of European descent—against the indigenous populations of many parts of the world. Third World governments, especially those which are perpetrating or permitting genocide, tend to accuse the West of self-righteous hypocrisy. The industrialized countries, they say, having ruthlessly destroyed and exploited people across the globe and become immensely rich in the process, can now afford to indulge a sentimental attachment to a few isolated tribes and demand that for their sake economic development—which would bring prosperity to millions—should be halted.

This criticism is understandable and just, but it does not alter the fact—which the developed world, from its own experience, is likely to recognize first—that many current development projects will prove catastrophic in the long-term and will fail to bring many of the benefits that are extravagantly claimed for them.

Scrutiny of Brazil's plans to 'colonize' the Amazon forest, for instance, reveals certain crucial discrepancies between the realities of the situation and the authorities' idealistic and much-publicized statements on the subject. The scheme will destroy the world's most complex

Claus Meyer/Transworld Feature Syndicate

(Above) Large-scale clearances of natural vegetation endanger many aboriginal societies. Brazil's plans to colonize the Amazon Basin is destroying the Indian population along with their homelands.

(Inset) The Sakuddei live in the dense rain forests of Siberut Island in Indonesia. A Filipino logging company has a concession in their area, so their traditional culture is unlikely to survive.

eco-system and natural scientists as well as anthropologists have predicted a disaster of global proportions. The scheme is advertized first and foremost as a cure for Brazil's chronic problems of poverty and over-population, but far from merely absorbing the unemployed now and for the foreseeable future the government estimates its plan will require a huge artificial increase in the population to some 900 million—about nine times the present number.

Those who do go out to the new frontier in the rush to exploit mineral resources will find that they are working not primarily for themselves or their people but for the companies which have bought mining and exploration concessions. Ironically, most of these are based in the United States and Europe, the very areas that have been accused of trying to meddle in Brazil's internal affairs when they have commented on the country's aboriginal policies.

Moreover, soil scientists and agricultural experts have found that the Amazon Basin offers very limited prospects for intensive Western-style farming and that if, as the authorities want, trees are felled and the land ploughed up for cultivation it will soon be exhausted. The present plans will in fact ensure that in 100 or 200 years' time Brazil will have no Amazon forest, no Indians and few resources, and will have multiplied its present problems of over-population and under-employment by at least nine times.

The alternative would be to proceed with the development of the Amazon at a rate to keep pace with natural population growth. On this more leisurely time-scale the damage done by mineral exploitation could be made good before the next part of the forest was tackled, and thus the wild-life and plant-life of the region would be far less disastrously affected. Moreover, the Indians, whose slash-and-burn agriculture probably represents the most efficient way of farming the forest, would have time to adjust to their changed circumstances and to share their skills and knowledge with the limited number of settlers that the Amazon could support.

A number of efforts have been made to persuade governments to implement more humane and realistic programmes and to protect aboriginal groups more effectively, but even among those who agree on the urgency of the situation and would like to help there are wide differences of opinion about what should actually be done. Some argue that efforts should be concentrated on preserving tribal cultures

Most of the Aborigines in Australia are restricted to reservations, where they are granted minimal living conditions. Recent political activity, particularly amongst the young, may improve their lot.

M. Vignes/John Hillelson Agency

(Above) North American Indians have regained their confidence in recent years. When Alcatraz prison closed in 1972, Indians occupied the island, demanding its return under an existing federal treaty.

(Below) Eskimo life has been transformed by modern technology. Evolved in a harsh environment, their culture has lost its meaning under the new conditions, leaving many Eskimos demoralized

Disappearing World/Granada Television

Boudewijn Weehuizen/Transworld Feature Syndicate

exactly as they are in order to maintain cultural diversity and provide future generations of anthropologists with the raw material from which to make their deductions about human society; others claim that this is a typically academic view, out of touch with real life, and would lead to the creation of a 'human zoo' whose inmates would never be able to make a choice as to their own future.

Whatever the merits of these various arguments, they have little practical relevance. The recent construction of a main road through the celebrated Xingu Indian reservation in Brazil shows that however carefully, intelligently and courageously people set out to protect tribes, the ultimate facts of aboriginal life and death are determined not by theoretical niceties but by the dynamics of the frontier. While American and European universities continue debating, the genocide goes on.

A number of small groups have been formed with the aim of helping threatened tribes, but most of them have collapsed. Their few members become disillusioned by squabbles, by lack of support—it is far easier to raise money for an endangered animal species, or even a museum, than for a near-extinct tribe— and by the refusal of governments to act even when experts agree on the policies that should be followed.

A few organizations have kept going against the odds, however, achieving results out of all proportion to their size. The International Work Group for Indigenous Affairs, for example, based in Denmark, publishes documents of a very high standard on the plight of particular aboriginal populations. Some of these, such as Mark Munzel's excellent account of the terrible treatment given the Ache Indians in Paraguay, have led to action by governments eager to avoid adverse publicity.

In Britain, Survival International, set up in the 1970s to fight for tribal societies throughout the world, has shown what can be done by intelligence, dedicated hard work, and only a small number of supporters. In 1974, after three years of research into the needs and special circumstances of a wide range of indigenous groups, Survival published a 'philosophy' which stated that its object was to 'try to provide aboriginal peoples with the opportunity to protect themselves'. This was to be achieved by securing title to their lands, so that they could be relieved, at least partially, from harassment, and ensuring that they understood enough of the national society and the wider world surrounding them to use European-style institutions in the fight for their own interests.

The first project, undertaken by Survival that same year in collaboration with the Committee for Indigenous Peoples,

concerned the Andoke tribe of Indians in Colombia. For years the Andoke had been harvesting rubber for a 'Rubber-Man' who paid them for their work in White goods and kept them, under the usual system, in a state of permanent— and worsening—debt. The government was about to give them a reservation in an area with little development potential, and under the leadership of a chief who had revived the tribe's traditional culture and its faith in itself they decided to ask, via a sympathetic anthropologist, for equipment to enable them to extract and sell rubber on their own account.

Survival and the CIP agreed to provide the £400 needed for the enterprise, and despite the 'Rubber-Man's' efforts to demoralize the Indians by telling them that the help would never arrive, they refused further goods from him and now hope to pay off their debt in two years. In addition to its obvious economic benefits, this comparatively small expenditure has brought incalculable gains in terms of independence, morale and self-respect.

Since this modest beginning Survival International has continued its policy of contacting and researching indigenous groups and talking to government officials and experts in order to develop really practicable schemes that relate directly to the needs of the peoples concerned. Sponsored projects, some of which have been totally or partially funded and are already under way, now include programmes in South America, Indonesia, Africa and elsewhere.

They all reflect Survival's constant concerns: safeguarding the health of tribes who might be decimated by White disease; securing title to tribal lands; helping peoples whose way of life is threatened to adapt to new subsistence patterns without losing their autonomy or their self-sufficiency; trying to improve the image of aboriginal groups in countries where they are despised and persecuted; and helping, through educational schemes and support for indigenous peoples' political associations, to make isolated or oppressed tribes aware of their situation and how it can be altered.

The growing awareness of the need for action has not been confined to Europe and the United States. Throughout the Americas and in other parts of the world there has been an astonishing re-awakening of cultural identity and pride among indigenous peoples themselves, and in a number of areas this has been expressed in the formation of political organizations and a more vociferous assertion of rights.

In October/November 1975, after years of work and repeated financial and technical setbacks, the Canadian National Indian Brotherhood succeeded in holding the first World Conference of Indigenous Peoples on an Indian reserve on Van-

couver Island. Representatives from the native populations of 19 countries met to discuss problems of common concern and possible approaches to solving them, and at the end of five days unanimously agreed to form themselves into a permanent organization, the World Council of Indigenous Peoples, to work for their joint interests.

Delegates were painfully aware, however, that poverty, ignorance, physical isolation and political oppression prevented those most in need from being represented at all. The Executive Council, under its President, George Manuel, has taken as its first task the accumulation of evidence on the situation of indigenous groups throughout the world for submission to the United Nations, where the WCIP has Non-Government Organization status. In this way, it is hoped, worldwide attention can be focussed on the plight of those peoples least able to help themselves, and pressure can be brought on the countries who are practising genocide most blatantly. In the longer term, the World Council aims to work for the return of control over their own destiny to the aboriginal peoples themselves.

Despite these encouraging signs, prospects for most indigenous people are still extremely bleak. With economic development accelerating in the relatively unexploited areas of the world, the last tribal societies are in grave danger of total extinction. Ultimately, their future can be secure only if we in the industrialized nations reduce our appetite for materials that can be acquired only by stealing their land and destroying their habitats; as the French anthropologist Robert Jaulin says: 'The solution to ethnocide will be found only within the framework of a modification of the West's attitude to the universe.'

Such a fundamental change, however, will be a long time coming, and its success, when it does come, will depend to a large extent on how well alternative attitudes have survived. If we act now, we can still give the remaining aboriginal societies the opportunity to adjust gradually and make real decisions as to their own futures. If we do nothing, by the end of the 1980s many—perhaps most—of them will have utterly disappeared, and it will probably be too late to save the remainder.

Western people will then finally have succeeded in eliminating the 'primitive' and we will all, in the long-term, be impoverished by the loss of some of our most precious human resources. If this does happen, we must not comfort ourselves with the reassuring old notion that it was inevitable anyway; we must realize that it was caused quite simply by our failure to respond, now, to a desperately urgent need. □